# The Outsiders

## Poets
## of
## Contemporary
## Ireland

BY
FRANK KERSNOWSKI

THE TEXAS CHRISTIAN UNIVERSITY PRESS
Fort Worth, Texas 76129

Library of Congress Catalog Card No. 74-21131
Manufactured in the United States of America

This book is dedicated to the memory of my father

Permission to reprint material, hereby acknowledged, has been given by the following:

From Samuel Beckett's POEMS IN ENGLISH (1961) by Grove Press; from Austin Clarke's COLLECTED POEMS (1936) by George Allen and Unwin Ltd.; from Seamus Heaney's DEATH OF A NATURALIST (1969) by Faber and Faber Ltd.; for F. Kersnowski's "The Fabulous Reality of Denis Devlin," which first appeared in THE SEWANEE REVIEW, 81 (1973), copyright by the University of the South, reprinted by permission of the editor; from Derek Mahon's NIGHT-CROSSING (1968) by Oxford University Press; from Ewart Milne's DIAMOND CUT DIAMOND (1950) by The Bodley Head; from A GARLAND FOR THE GREEN (1962) by Ewart Milne; from James Simmons's BALLAD OF A MARRIAGE by Queen's University Festival, Belfast.

There they are then: Kinsella, Montague, O'Grady, all under thirty-five. They are not the whole of young Irish verse. The picture will be more complete when we have volumes from Pearse Hutchinson, Richard Weber and James Liddy. They are the generation which succeeds that of which Valentin Iremonger in the South and Roy McFadden in the North were the most distinguished. Somewhere in between came Anthony Cronin — a curious evidence of how late Auden came to Ireland. Our poets nowadays are far more hep, and they deserve critics less kindly and more rigorous than myself.

John Jordan in *THE DOLMEN MISCELLANY*, 1962

# Contents

IX. Poetry of Outsiders

### CHAPTER I

# Introduction

The Irish poets who have reached maturity since World War II have seldom received attention and never of the kind given their predecessors. Most critics seem to have accepted Auden's dirge for Irish poetry upon the death of Yeats: "The vessel of Irish poetry is emptied."[1] The greatness of writers during the Irish Literary Renaissance remains unquestioned. And the settling of graves and books has caused no significant changes in evaluation: between the polarity of Yeats and Joyce, the systematizers, are ranked their contemporaries — but seldom their survivors. The writers growing into the twentieth century, as Yeats said, had their childhood beliefs destroyed by the Victorian scientists.[2] These writers, in their own time, formulated complex ontological systems which assured the undying dignity of man. All would return. Their confidence seems distant and foreign to many people who remember the organized and methodical devastation of World War II, who were stunned by the mushroom cloud crown of the intellect, who have seen the dwindling glory of the Irish revolutionary spirit.

The writer of the Renaissance had seen life in mists from bogs and in clouds of smoke stemming from the Irish tobacco they affected. The writers immediately after World War II almost rejected Ireland as a subject. Except that it was their habitat and inheritance, they would have ignored it. In fact, their efforts were to establish internationalism as a doctrine. Perhaps because most of Ireland had not taken part in the great conflagration on the Continent, the writers turned from distinctly Irish problems and became absorbed in the problems of post-war Europe and America. The injustices done to Blacks in America, Jews in Germany,

1

were frequent subjects; and the tinker's poverty, the Church's domination, were ignored, as was the growing problem of Northern Ireland. More important than their subject was the approach. Man was no longer an abstraction, capable of "profane perfection."[3] He was flawed and temporary. This, then, is the essential belief of the contemporary Irish writer, hardly a suitable center for a coterie. Such a gathering would have to be called group therapy and might well become a substitute for writing.

Among the contemporaries some gathering together has taken place, but only Austin Clarke has attempted to bring past patterns to present problems. He at one time gathered young to his house as did Yeats and AE when they held their famous evenings. But Clarke was too gentle a man to possess the charismatic arrogance that seems necessary for literary dictators. AE, of whom most of the contemporaries speak with as much kindness as they do anger for Yeats, was able to exist without the arrogance. One wonders if he could have without the contrary of Yeats to turn the young in his path. Also, Clarke's mind remained wed to a problem that does not exist for the younger writers: the dilemma of a man pulled by fondness for the traditional past and the excitement of the rapid modern world. The writer today cannot use the past as a pleasant asylum, for there he finds stories and writers who seem as disturbed as he is.

However, seen from the vantage point of hindsight, even such an avowed internationalist as Anthony Cronin has always been consciously Irish, but in a much different way than was true of the figures of the Literary Renaissance. He thought of himself, even then, as part of a tradition, as is shown by his membership in the small band that in 1954 made the first Bloomsday walk. With him were Patrick Kavanagh, Brian O'Nolan (Myles naGopaleen), and John Ryan (one of the editors of *Envoy*).[4] In their way, these men tried to bring recognition to Irish literature, past and present, just as much as Yeats did. But the walls of the literary edifice were falling just as do those of the lovely Georgian houses in Dublin. Tradition demanded the return of Finn to shore up the ruin. Neither Finn, nor Joyce, nor Yeats was unavoidably present. One is inclined to say about all of post-war Ireland what Brian Moore said of Belfast when he contrasted its plainness with the glories of Dublin: "Writers, poets, painters? Alas, dear Eustace, we have not the vocation. Respectable craftsmen can be discovered in all three pursuits, but the city has produced no poet who strides the world's stage, no novelist to distract American Ph.D.'s from their Joycean researches in the banlieux of Dublin."[5] For a serious writer to accept such a view of himself could be stultifying. Fortunately, the new writers have learned to live with the memory of the past, without letting it dominate their present.

The internationalists consciously freed themselves from a literary tradition embodied in writers of megalithic reputations. Their doctrine became the appraisal of their own writing and that of all others in essentially aesthetic and psychological terms rather than in nationalistic terms. Of course, this was very much the approach of professional litterateurs in the fifties. In Ireland, the task was too formidable. The country certainly would not support such radicalism, and academia had so little autonomy that it could not.

Internationalism, which is still somewhat important in Irish writing, gave the young writer an opportunity to detach himself from a smothering tradition. In time, a distance from the past was achieved and the contemporary writer could discern the parts of the culture and tradition of Ireland which had relevance for him. And having made his journey away from the founding fathers of modern Irish literature, he could then do, or re-do, some of the work they had done. Perhaps the lapse of time alone would have freed the new writer from the influence of the immediate past, but the effort of the writers to discover themselves as part of a live and relevant culture is striking. They have existed in what Bergson called real, as opposed to chronological, time; for accomplishment and growth measure them, not years.[6]

Ireland for the new writers in general has little resemblance to the country of the Anglo-Irish, which dominated the understanding of Yeats and his friends. Some of that world still exists, but the writers do not see it as important to their identity. Instead, they concern themselves, in their writing, with the lives and beliefs of the native Irish. The range of the subject extends from Clarke's rather archaic attack on the Irish Catholic Church to Devlin and Montague's admiration for the unpretentious country

3

people who still live in the tide pools of history where old cour-
tesies and simple faith have currency. In between are many important members for the Irish literary scene: sensitive and educated people of middle-class families. These people, so similar to
the literati of all western countries, differ from others in that they
have an ancient literary tradition and a language which is important to them. These give them a fixity in place and time seldom
available to their contemporaries in other countries. Though
Dublin and, increasingly, Belfast are firmly established as the
centers of art and publishing, the new writer often comes from
small towns or the country. Coming to the centers, he finds
himself shaped by a more sophisticated culture; but he bears scant
resemblance to the Anglo-Irish gentlemen shaped by the Literary
Renaissance. That time is past.

Much like the poetry in Britain and America, that written by
the contemporary Irish is strongly confessional and conversational. Their concern with image and the immediate presentation of
experience, either psychological or physical, makes the traditional metaphoric structure of poetry tenuous. Metaphor necessitates reference to a system of values outside the experience itself,
and none of the new poets has formulated a coherent system.
Perhaps because of the pervasive presence of the past, few of the
poets are able to avoid shaping their experiences. Most of the
contemporary writers deal with the difficulty of being human,
especially in a country stumbling into the last half of the twentieth
century. They may praise the past, but as a contrast to present day
practices that they find offensive. They have selected what they
wanted from the past and attempted to bring it into the overtly
complex life of a contemporary man, but few of them have
accepted their predecessors' ethic or life style. To do that would
be to risk turning poetry into a tourist attraction or a museum
piece.

However, the attention paid to places in the contemporary
poetry securely ties it to that of the past. Traditionally, places of
historical or legendary importance have figured largely in Irish
poetry. One can, of course, find concern with local color in the
writings of all cultures; but in contemporary times the nostalgic or
evocative quality is stronger among the Irish poets than any other.

The reason for this characteristic may be the influence of earlier writing, by Joyce especially. More probably, the poets present a quality that is alive and constant in Irish culture. Monuments and places often assume anthropomorphic value in Ireland, and in time even a stranger finds himself understanding.

No unified literary movements have brought Irish poetry to its present state, but writers of *similar* goals have frequently found themselves published by the same periodical or press. A very uncentralized development has taken place, aided probably more than impeded by the familial society of literary Ireland. Family feuds of the bitterest kind do happen. Because of these and the factors of age, religion, ancestry, and politics, clusters of writers have often paid a loose allegiance to a publication. And as happens with all writing in all countries, the publication usually becomes the organ of a few kindred writers who may even consider themselves a movement. But more often, the writers who are not part of the editorial staff will simply be associated with the publication because their writing is appreciated and published. In Ireland, at least, periodicals necessarily die for lack of support; and the writers must move to other editors. So no single publication has dominated the growth of the contemporary writing. In tracing the development of contemporary Irish poetry, then, one examines the significance of publications which have drawn groups of writers together, however loosely, as well as the careers of individual poets.

*CHAPTER II*

# *Envoy*

*Envoy* was the periodical which began the internationalist movement in Ireland after World War II. But as is always true among the Irish writers, no venture begins without approaching past literary wars or ends without creating new ones. The particular issue at this time was the memory and presence of figures of the Irish Literary Renaissance, especially the poets who gathered around Yeats. Their self-conscious Irishism, modeled upon Anglo-Irish principles, began to cloy, then enrage.

Though internationalism was the guide, old animosities quickly became relevant. Austin Clarke, for instance, was a reminder of the era before them; he became the "enemy."[1] In part, this animosity can be explained by the term "generation gap," in part by the difference in life styles. The *Envoy* people were known for their extravagant, even riotous, behavior. Clarke is, and seems to have long been such, a calm and decorous man. Also, a serious personal quarrel between Kavanagh and Clarke never seems to have healed. This last point needs to be remembered. Kavanagh's own writing had no bearing on the internationalist understanding. His articles were concerned with Irish problems, and his role as a contributing editor was to attack "the establishment," dead and living.

The two-pronged approach of *Envoy*, attack and internationalism, did not succeed in liberating any of the contributing editors from the oppressiveness of their literary past. These editors, except for Kavanagh, have never been prolific: Valentin Iremonger has two volumes of beautiful lyrics; Anthony Cronin's verse, fiction, and criticism appear with increasing infrequency; John Ryan, a generous and well-informed man, has only recently returned to editing. But this periodical, for all its outrageousness, began the process of freeing contemporary Irish literature from the control of the past by showing writers that other approaches to life and art exist. *Envoy* separated the Irish writer, briefly, from a simple identification with Ireland and substituted a psychological understanding for a national one. Then the real and valuable qualities of Irishness could be seen. However, the periodical was not totally ameliorative in its effect. Patrick Kavanagh developed an identity just as artificially Irish as the one he attacked. Even today many writers and would-be writers play his role, use his excuses.

*Patrick Kavanagh*          Patrick Kavanagh discussed in each issue of *Envoy* the nature of Irish art and his hopes for the future. Essentially, he saw Irish art as bound by critics who could only be destructive because they viewed contemporary art by outmoded standards and by narrow-minded nationalism. Brian Boydell contended that this provinciality would cause the Irish to "lock ourselves in the bathroom (having first made sure that we have turned off the water lest we should be tempted to benefit from any cleansing influence from outside)."[2] All of the editors paid serious concern to writing in England, America, and the Continent. Articles on and reprints of works by Anton Chekhov, Gerard de Nerval, Gertrude Stein, André Gide, and Henry Miller appeared. And Kavanagh in a column called "Kavanagh's Diary" wrote of his travels and his reading.

Kavanagh, for all his international flourishes, began and remained a poet bound by the narrowness he despised. *Tarry Flynn*, a novel about the youth of a writer, shows the source of his limitations: the young man in the novel is like a lyrical Jude; but his weakness is love for the Irish countryside, not overwhelming passion. Never was Kavanagh able to resist the opportunity to write a pastoral poem, such as "The Goat of Slieve Donard":

> I saw an old white goat on the slope of Slieve Donard,
> Nibbling daintily at the herb leaves that grow in
>     the crevasses. . . .[3]

The poem is deft, though the maudlin tone that will dominate his later poetry already appears. To explain blatantly, with
agrarian metaphors, an obvious truth occurs repeatedly in
Kavanagh's poetry. The accuracy of the view is unquestionable,
but naiveté in phrasing effectively destroys the force of the truth.
The continuous and obvious search for a metaphor at times has
pleasing, though partial, results. In "Tinker's Wife" he describes
the woman: "Her face had streaks of care / Like wires across it."[4]
The woman becomes strongly present in these two lines, but the
rest of the poem cannot support description so consciously calling
attention to itself.

Then, too, Kavanagh frequently dealt in artless terms that
suggest cleverness. In his early poems, such as "After May," the
device lacks even offense, relying totally in artlessness: "Sweet
May is gone, and now must poets croon / The praises of a rather
stupid June."[5] A poem in which he deals with a traditional lyric
theme without any ironic device suggests why he may have
mocked lyricism:

> November is come and I wait for you still
> O nimble-footed nymph who slipped me when
> I sighted you among some silly men
> And charged you with the power of my will.[6]

Too much romanticism and sentiment force his poems into being
mementoes of Ireland, picture postcard illustrations.

"The Great Hunger," which may well be Kavanagh's best
poem, combines his irony and pastoral sentiment into a comment
on lives wasted in drudgery and celibacy. The obvious searching
for metaphor remains, but his sincerity often lifts his comment to
the level of sensitive art:

> Turn over the weedy clods and tease out the tangled skeins
> What is he looking for there?
> He thinks it is a potato, but we know better
> Than his mud-gloved fingers probe in this insensitive
>       hair.[7]

This poem, more than any other, made Kavanagh generally important. The offence it gave, because of its truth and directness,
caused him difficulty, in the way of threats. But it also called

attention to his talent, a talent so unrestrained that even in this poem the falling into poetic banality was inescapable:

> Health and wealth and love he too dreamed of in May
> As he sat on the railway slope and watched the
>     children of the place
> Picking up a primrose here and a daisy there —
> They were picking up life's truth singly.[8]

The whole poem is discursive, a quality quite antithetical to what Kavanagh had praised about the poet Auden: "Auden, like all the great ones, is all sensation, all pictures, action."[9] The poem, even if the overt philosophizing were deleted, would still not be "all sensation." "The Great Hunger" is a long, ironic Irish in-joke. Whenever anyone in Ireland refers to the great hunger, he means the potato famine that existed in Ireland from 1845 to 1848. Ireland never recovered from the loss of population through the ensuing starvation and emigration. Kavanagh's poem is about the Irishman's hunger for life, especially the carnal. As such, it is an important comment on the effect of the puritanical Irish Catholic Church on the population.

Kavanagh's poems about the sterility and decay of Ireland suggest the guidance of Joyce. But unlike Joyce, Kavanagh did not become a permanent exile. He spent most of his life in Ireland and nourished the bitterness and despair that is the subject of *Dubliners* and *A Portrait of the Artist as a Young Man*. "The Defeated" is Kavanagh's basic, and ambivalent, condemnation of his country:

> Drink up, drink up, the troughs of Paris and
> London are no better than your own,
> Joyce learned that bitterly in a foreign land.
> Don't laugh, there is no answer to that one!
> Outside this pig-sty life deteriorates,
> Civilization dwindles.[10]

Censuring all, even life itself, yet Kavanagh holds out a sop to Ireland. Perhaps, if Joyce had not freed himself from a country that he thought resembled a sow that eats its own farrow, he would also have found his art limited to diatribe. Kavanagh remained an Irishman railing at the exile, as in "Joyce's Ulysses":

> The children take delight in levelling the city,
> Violently tear down the walls,
> Screeching from the steps of a ruin
> Where a broken milk bottle rolls.[11]

However, Kavanagh's bitterness is so all-encompassing that he refuses to admit that anyone else might have found nourishment in the writings of Joyce. In doggerel he reflects:

> Who killed James Joyce?
> I, said the commentator,
> I killed James Joyce
> For my graduation.[12]

Kavanagh did not limit his attacks to the critic, the interloper. He was equally astringent with other high writers.

"The Paddiad" rejects Yeats, Joyce, O'Casey, the poetry of bogs and mists, tourist attractions, and government supported poetry. Kavanagh struck with harshness in all directions in which he saw success, and he did so knowingly. For him, life could not have a center of affirmation, leaving him only a perimeter of condemnation:

> *The Great Hunger* is concerned with the woes of the poor. A true poet is selfish and implacable. A poet merely states the position and does not care whether his words change anything or not. *The Great Hunger* is tragedy and Tragedy is underdeveloped Comedy, not fully born. Had I stuck to the tragic thing in *The Great Hunger* I would have found many powerful friends.
>
> But I lost my messianic compulsion. I sat on the bank of the Grand Canal in the summer of 1955 and let the water lap idly on the shores of my mind. My purpose in life was to have no purpose.[13]

Especially at this time in the twentieth century, when all wait for a new universal purpose to occur, such a view appeals widely. I found no Irish writers bothered by Kavanagh's lack of direction. If such a life as Kavanagh described led to happiness, or even contentment, it would be desirable. However, he recorded the unhappiness of his life in maudlin, self-pitying verse.

Kavanagh continues to exist as an important force, for he was instrumental in changing the contemporary writers' view of their literary past. His attacks in *Envoy* on Yeats and Higgins, after both were dead, may have been excessive and often offensive. But they

11

were needed then, just as much as they had been when the men were alive. After the impassioned attacks of Kavanagh, complemented by the approach of *Envoy*, there seemed to be a bit more ease in Irish writing. No longer did writers feel totally bound by the taste and message of the past.

Perhaps, the separation / liberation from the past could not have occurred without such harshness and bitterness. But Kavanagh's attacks did not make him the medium of such passions. They were basic to his character long before, and he set the tone of the censure. He was caught between memory of a childhood he could neither reject nor accept and the actuality of an adult life in literary circles that must have been far different from what a romantic young countryman expected. Result: sentimental reflection / rejection of the past and nostalgia for the past. But Kavanagh never made the opposites work for him. Always he was torn and always bled in verse.

As a young man, he read much, published a little, and then came to know the gentler figures of the Irish Literary Renaissance, such as AE. His shock at seeing that the baseness and opportunism of the farmer, the business man, existed among writers can be forcefully felt in "The Paddiad." That writers were different from what he expected from reading books was not, though, as constant a theme as his own lack of success, often recorded with musings on his loneliness, as in "Bank Holiday." Of his many workings on this theme, "The Same Again" comes closest to working poetically:

I have my friends, my public and they are waiting
For me to come again as their one and only bard
With a new statement that will repay all the waitment
While I was hitting the bottle hard.
I know it is not right to be light and flippant
There are people in the streets who steer by my star.
There was nothing they could do but view me while
   I threw
Back large whiskeys in the corner of a smoky bar
And if only I would get drunk it wouldn't be so bad
With a pain in my stomach I wasn't even comic
Swallowing every digestive pill to be had.[15]

12

Here Kavanagh evokes, as he can do so well, the Irish pub. But the self-pitying irony in speaking of his "public" as if it really existed runs throughout the poem. Such a confessional poem probably could be nothing other than maudlin verse, for Kavanagh's pain and disappointment were too great to be marshalled into something other than a poem appropriate for quoting nostalgically in Irish pubs. There he is remembered, and some perhaps even accept the ironic rejection of failure in this poem.

Kavanagh did have moments, even late in life, when he must have believed in the reality of his talent and of the waste of his life. At such times, he changes from self-pity to vituperative attack on poets who have become highly thought of, who have a public. Speaking of himself in "Sensational Disclosures!":

> He could disburse
> A faulosity of verse,
> Could swallow without dodgery
> Ted Hughes' menagerie,
> He often spat forth
> Lions of more wrath.[16]

Such an attack can only be tolerable, or successful, when done with as much art and craft as possessed by the poets who are being attacked. This poem never rises above doggerel.

Kavanagh's irreverence was needed to free the Irish artist from the burden of literary giants who came before him and from his countrymen who never ceased wanting to see a flattering picture of themselves. But Kavanagh found an audience who would accept without question his poems, pub-wit made public, and never effectively went beyond that small group. Perhaps, he could not; for his talent was a minor one. And in Dublin such limitations can gain fame through failure.

*Valentin Iremonger*

Valentin Iremonger and Anthony Cronin, the other two contributing editors of *Envoy*, echoed Kavanagh's theory of internationalism. Perhaps, since neither stayed in Ireland, neither allowed condemnation of others to become the bulk of his writing.

Iremonger is quite aware that continual satisfaction of the audience's expectations has made the Irish writer a predictable and provincial being. "Eloquence," never to be at a loss for a word, Iremonger sees as "The greatest Irish fault." Since the choice of words is too often wrong, even works by such masters as Yeats are "invalidated." Also, the Irish writer has traditionally treated material which Iremonger refuses to accept as relevant to his own writing: "the unusual, the colorful, the odd, arranged for the titilation of the reflexes of a non-Irish public without much regard for the artistic merits of the contents."[17] As all of his poems show, however, Iremonger did not reject the relevance of the social and cultural entity of Ireland to his art.

Even his recent poems illustrate this awareness of himself as Irish. In "An Old Tune" he evokes a scene that is Irish and people who are simply human:

Jane Brown had red hair that dazzled
The boys in Sandymount when she was even eight.
Going from school, all would be eager
Politely to see her to the garden gate. . . .[18]

This poem illustrates Iremonger's own explanation of how the Irish writer is to avoid insularity: "Are our own paltry problems of our relationship with our country (problems common to every writer no matter what his nationality) not to be sublimated into the more general problem of our relationship with the whole human community."[19] Like Iremonger, the writers of the Irish Revival also saw the universal through the immediate; but unlike them Iremonger has not seen huge god-like figures, making human vice and value paltry. He and the rest of the contemporary Irish poets have avoided the grand purposes of such a writer as Yeats, who could only express his love for his daughter in terms of a cataclysmic social change:

Once more the storm is howling, and half hid
Under this cradle-hood and coverlid
My child sleeps on. There is no obstacle
But Gregory's wood and one bare hill
Whereby the haystack- and roof-levelling wind,
Bred on the Atlantic can be stayed;

And for an hour I have walked and prayed
Because of the great gloom that is in my mind.[20]

Yeats's poem contrasts the growing democratic government with the waning aristocratic one. Never does the particular lead Iremonger in such a direction. Even in "An Old Tune" he avoided the grand. Jane Brown could easily have become Cathleen ni Houlihan, the personification of Ireland. Instead, she is a girl become a woman whom every man has known and loved.

Robert Graves is the one Irish poet Iremonger mentioned as showing contemporary poets a valid approach to their culture. Graves's concern for language produces a poetry with "no trace of Irishness," but it is also outside the mainstream of English poetry. Ignoring the poetry of doubt and anxiety Graves wrote just after World War I, Iremonger emphasized Graves's return to Celtic myth and nature poetry to implement his writing poetry of myth and magic.[21] "Spring Stomp" shows Iremonger's use of myth and magic:

So, love, let you come dancing
Down the jazzy lanes of spring,
Through the ragtime green of meadows
By the high cliff's muted brink.
Let's swing it by the river
To the torch-song of the water
While yet our sinews answer
The off-beat's hot-licked pause.[22]

He writes here of the return of the goddess as Graves did in "To Juan at the Winter Solstice," but with a noticeable difference in diction.[23] Both poets have equated love, woman, and the seasons. Graves, though, has increasingly freed his diction of all possible contemporary reference. Iremonger has used contemporary slang almost to the point of affectation.

Iremonger's consciously contemporary diction resembles his approach to Irishness: man is forever and everywhere the same; only his referents are different. Since World War II man has new referents. "Soldier from the Wars" describes a man who has come back to Ireland to find peace and home:

> May he survive unscathed the Dunkirk of middle-age
> And cardiac decay, the Crete of married life,
> The Peloponnese-like archipelagoes of children,
>     to fish lazily
> In the reaches of quiet old age.[24]

This eclectic mixing of times and places succeeds in turning all to metaphors of man. And man is his subject, whether he looks at his own time or Swift's, as he does in "The Choice."[25]

Always Iremonger works the same themes: growing up, emotional exuberance and awkwardness, the conflict of man and society, the irrevocable past. The last is especially significant because earlier writers founded their approach to life and art on a belief in the inevitable return of a glorious, though mythical, past. Even the wars from 1916 to 1927 only served to convince them of the nearness of a new birth. Valentin Iremonger, among others, recorded the effects by writing of the common experiences of man caught in the inevitable movement of time and denied the older belief of the necessity of heroic and haughty individuality. "A Pane of Glass" portrays the citizen of the new world as locked away from his desires by job and responsibility, the latter providing the rationalization of the former. As an accountant sits in his office writing a threatening letter to his child's schoolmaster, he pauses to watch men working on the street outside:

> What but to break the glass and unhampered let me chip
> My life to the required smooth even shape
> And let the roadmaster, if he so wishes, balance
> The account of his days and threaten all the bosses.[26]

When he looks at life as a process, he quite often does so with some regret for his youth that is gone, aligning him with the contemporary cult of the young:

> Gone, now, the adolescent swagger and closed
> The book of my youth, ruled, and a trial
> Balance extracted for my future use.[27]

Iremonger seems essentially concerned with writing poetry that is relevant to his audience yet based on universal and timeless themes. He is, however, bound to a poetic that though beautiful is of the past. The difficulty, and obscurity, of some of the later poets is not to be found in his writing. Unlike them, he does not turn through mazes of introspection or present objectively the signposts of his culture. Nor does he seem to have the literary ambition of Anthony Cronin, the third poet editor of *Envoy*.

*Anthony Cronin*   Cronin's most important discussion of the writer in Ireland was published in *The Bell*, after the death of *Envoy*. Ireland, unlike other countries, did not have a "movement" composed of young writers who ignored elders with whom they disagreed and published their own work in their own journals. Ireland is too small for writers to avoid one another, and it does not have "enough young writers to make a movement."[28] Predictably, his solution is exile. Like many Irish writers before him, he moved to London and charted his own struggle with that literary world. His novel, *The Life of Reilly*, describes the life of the young writer. He is a curious outsider to members of movements, of which there are plenty, and soon becomes the prey-protégé of Irishmen who are parodying themselves. He did not go in arrogance as did Yeats or with cunning as did Joyce, nor did he go for the same reasons.

Cronin's explanation of the necessity of exile is that of the internationalists of *Envoy* and *The Bell*. These men said, and some believed, that the rebirth of the Irish writer could only be effected by his adoption of techniques and attitudes foreign to Irish literature and by the rejection of a debilitating and discouraging past. Commenting on the young writer in Ireland, Cronin synthesized all that had been said, though he alone spoke of movements as necessary and exile as inevitable. He is eager to be a writer and dead-tired of being expected to care about Ireland's continued lack of success since the establishment of the Free State in 1921.[29]

Cronin also mentions the failure of the revolution to produce a country even faintly resembling the one hoped for by seven hundred years of patriots and martyrs. The lack of affluence, the absence of social welfare, the continued separation of Northern and Southern Ireland, the great power of the Church keep Ireland

17

from entering the post-war world. Yet the Irish find this new world fascinating. They are aware of the passage of time in and out of their country. Although they may laughingly point to an old man in tweeds and bowler tottering into the Shelbourne during Horse Show Week as "the last of a dying breed, an Anglo-Irish gentleman," they have yet to improve the country they took from him.[30]

The criticism of Anthony Cronin, unlike his novel, is distinguishable as Irish only because of the frequent reference to Irish writing. Neither it nor his poetry draws from native sources. Frequently, the same themes occur in both his prose and poetry:

> He grew into exile slowly,
> With pride and remorse,
> In some ways better than his begetters,
> In others worse.[31]

The highly discursive quality of Cronin's criticism is not found in his poetry, and what in prose was internationalism in poetry becomes indistinctiveness. Surprising, too, is the absence in the poetry of any direct association with the present time.

Donald Carroll said Cronin's volume of poems "introduced Auden into the fraternity of Irish letters."[32] A similarity between the two poets does exist, but the differences between them are even stronger. Cronin writes poems about ideas; and Auden presents ideas through images, as he did in "O Where Are You Going" and "In Praise of Limestone."[33] Auden is a mythopoeic poet, a trait not to be found in Cronin.

Cronin's tone in all his writing is that of the professional literary man. He is analytical and *au courant* because the particular mode of writing he approves of is intellectual and experimental. As an editor of *Envoy* he added a needed professionalism. He and Iremonger aided in passing on the care of the young writer from dead *Envoy* to still living *The Bell*. *The Bell* of October, 1951, was devoted to the young writer. The comments by the writers were largely concerned with explaining the end of *Envoy*. One interesting exception was John Montague's. He, with Roy McFadden, is one of the important poets of contemporary Ireland who published in but was not of *Envoy*. Though they have alliances in the

South, these two really belong to the North — thus to a community very different from that developing in Eire. Montague briefly described the limited worth of *The Bell* and perhaps that of the community:

> *The Bell* has developed an argumentative complex, and by constantly keeping in mind the social angle or problem has tended to lead writing away from its real purpose at the present time, the imaginative and honest expression of the writer's own problems, not those of his sickening community, though the one will indirectly be reflected in the other.[34]

Some of his censure must touch *Envoy*, which avowedly intended to raise Ireland from its doldrums by attack and unflattering contrast with other countries.

*Pearse Hutchinson*

Pearse Hutchinson in his life and writing represents much that made *Envoy* both necessary and important. Finding the regimen and comformity of UCD unattractive and valueless, he left academia for the much more unstable world of the professional writer. *The Bell* and *Irish Writing* were the only two significant native markets for his, and others', writing; and they were edited by men with whom he was acquainted. On the other hand, *Envoy* had Anthony Cronin and John Ryan, close friends from McDaid's. *Envoy*, then, provided the new and rebellious with a receptive and friendly market.[35]

In his first volume, *Tongue Without Hands*, Hutchinson made his separation from traditional society a central theme. Not having the security of numbers that so many of the young have today, the poet of the late forties and early fifties would skirt his real subject not so much to avoid censure as to have some base on which to build. "Petition to Release" expresses his resentment towards a society that chained and rejected him as "different":

> I don't know who the hell could get me to work,
> a black boy goes boasting beside Mayaro Bay.[36]

Resentment is the one word that describes the tone of the poems in this volume, resentment not only towards those who would shackle life but poetry as well:

A self-styled misanthrope, who wrote perfect pentameters,
but was not in many ways truly conformist,
wanted to build the kind of tower that used to be of ivory
in the days when ivory was cheap.
He couldn't afford it, so he used
black brick instead.
Nevertheless, he passed an Act of Will whereby the tower
would be described as ivory;
he was not so much in pursuit of truth
as in flight from those in flight from it.[37]

Even the man who is willing to conform, tacitly at least, cannot be left alone. Public pressure forces him to abandon his retreat, to avoid direct confrontation.

Pearse Hutchinson and others at the time of *Envoy* found themselves tied to Ireland (even more specifically to Dublin), which angered and repulsed them by its middle-class ethic and mentality. So Pearse Hutchinson went to Spain for ten years, with one recess in Ireland. While away he translated some poems from the Catalan, for which he has been justly and highly praised. Drawn by the story of romantic Spain, bull fights, mantillas, he stayed because of his understanding of people who struggle, or do not have the strength to, against oppression. He may be one of the people in "Travel Notes":

Two foreigners in a century,
perhaps, break through to a nation's core:
to them: honour . . .[38]

The desire of Irish writers just after World War II to achieve an internationalist's identification of self forms this poem.

The inability to be in cultural exile is so strong among all the Irish that one can understand why *Envoy* did not neglect the country but strove to make it more enlightened, more European. Ireland, especially Dublin, is very like a too attentive parent and necessitates a love-hate relationship if one is to avoid total destruction of the self. Even the most resentful of artists is drawn back to the almost comforting separation of the country from the complex and dangerous world outside. In "Korea" he reflects on Dublin:

> Lemon tea, peanut butter, and cinnamon toast.
> Then, at two in the morning, we left the pleasant
>   room.
> Liquorless, gay, and perfect, we sang down Merrion
>   Row.
> It seemed as if Rhonabwy's Age had come.
>
> At Stephen's Green, for some reason, we bought a
>   paper.
> The scare headlines persuaded us we and all men had lost.
> In a snack-bar, scared, we drank rat-coloured coffee.
> After lemon tea, peanut butter, and cinnamon toast.[39]

This poem has very little that Pearse Hutchinson would consider shaping, the changing of a private experience to a public one.[40] But it does reveal his tie to a particular idea of Ireland: gay, spontaneous. The freedom offered by residing in a politically irrelevant country cannot be lightly valued. Finding Ireland's foreign involvements slight and her internal ones extremely forboding, the poets during the time of *Envoy* attempted to arouse the intelligentsia. But almost all of these were looking forward to exile or playing the current role of Irishman as rancourous gadfly who buzzed happily in his favorite pub — usually McDaid's.

So the serious poet, like Pearse Hutchinson, shaped his writing away from the immediate and personal experience of the man within the culture, that being generally irrelevant to everyone. Instead, he asserted that men are intrinsically the same everywhere yet culturally distinguishable. As is so obvious, with Pearse Hutchinson, the awareness of Irishness had been waiting for the support of the many. He first published a poem in Irish in 1954, and in 1968 published a book of poems in Irish. This growing concern does not indicate a return to cultural insularity. For him to write in Irish is just as much part of his understanding of himself in international terms as to write in Spanish.[41]

*Expansions*, the title of his second volume, indicates acceptance of his identity within his culture, as does his return to

Ireland. In "Questions" he equates the Irish and the Spanish: both have been subjected to linguicide (the destruction of Irish and Catalonian), and both have become timorous:

> In young reluctant ears, bullied, bellowed,
> it came like that: bared of music
> like a writer of words; a dried fountain
> with small pale lizards
> pretending to be chameleons
> scurrying about on the concrete.[42]

A mask almost covers the actual subject here, but in other poems the thing itself appears without metaphor or explanation. "Friday in a Branch Post-Office" has old people in a queue redeeming stamps sent them by relatives. Neglect and loneliness are to be seen among the old of every country, but the poem becomes immediately topical in the last two lines: "We don't need a statue of CúChulain / in our Branch Post-Office."[43] The statue of this hero in the G.P.O. was intended to remind all Irishmen of the heroic sacrifice made in 1916 which made Ireland free and proud. The old are a depressing contradiction. The young as well find Ireland a country fallen far from the noble promises of the revolutionaries. In "Fleadh Cheoil" a young musician visiting his home in Clare after working in England proclaims a new independence:

> 'You know what I think of it,
> over there?
> Over there, you're free'.[44]

In each case, Hutchinson has reproached his country for rejecting and repressing individuals, for disallowing love as an answer.

The theme of separation from the general community because he is deemed "weird" or different is carried over from *Tongue Without Hands*, but the later poems generally avoid the disguised subject. "Freakspiel" and "Speaking to Some" present the outcast:

> and heard, after you've asked the way and been told,
> with enormous courtesy and meticulous truth,
> as you moved away the snigger bursting out . . . .[45]

With each example of rejection comes his fear and their hatred of that which is different, anyone who varies:

> How long can he like this burg
> where the glic may call you
> 'pathological'
> for challenging words like
> 'nigger'?[46]

The anguished confessional of a Creeley or a Plath is absent here and seldom occurs in contemporary Irish poetry — especially not among those who grew through *Envoy*, which cleared the air, and into *Arena*, which attempted to give Ireland a conscience based on love and tolerance.

To gauge the success of *Envoy* one must employ standards other than longevity and prosperity, for it was short-lived and probably did not pay its way, but was, nevertheless, a success. *Envoy* was the first significant stage in the reshaping of Irish literature and is important as the immediate source of what in other times would have become a movement. Of course, the actual sources are part of the whole development of modern Irish literature. Yeats and those who followed or came after him insisted upon avoidance of narrow provincialism. The men who founded *Envoy*, Kavanagh especially, had long been engaged in contests with people who expected literature to provide propaganda. And for him, the Irish Renaissance was propaganda.

### CHAPTER III

# *Arena*

*Arena* entered into a spirited attack on Irish provincialism, but with a complete avant-garde commitment. Avant-garde as here used is limited to Norman Podhoretz's definition: "The movement of formal experimentation."[1] The second issue of *Arena* contained a description of the editorial policy that seems applicable to the first as well as the last three issues:

> The editors do not regard themselves as ivory tower tenants or lily-holders, but a group who know beauty without humanity is not acceptable. Asked for a dogma, we would say we believe in the coming of the bards: who deny Narcissus, who synthesize the mass-thought, and who utter in public what should be said.[2]

In several ways the same statement is often made: to be human is to acknowledge union with all humanity, to be kind and loving to everyone else is therefore a human necessity, to speak openly of any part of the total unity is to be good, to reject the security of labels which separate people from one another is to attempt to be good. Perhaps even more important, *Arena* turned from Ireland even more than did *Envoy*. Essays on racial discrimination in America took the place of needed examination and censure of Irish ways.

*Michael Hartnett*

Understandably, some writers for *Arena* would, in rejecting prescriptive Irishness, affirm total Irishness. In "Documents for Paul Potts," Michael Hartnett wrote, "The true ubermensch is the mononationalist, the raceless."[3] The rest of the prose and poetry in this section presents the unpleasantness of discrimination against Negroes and Jews and suggests a causal

25

relationship between it and the war that culminated in Hiroshima and Nagasaki. Michael Hartnett is frequently concerned with such specific examples of inhumanity and also frequently models his poetry on the Japanese. Perhaps the light and brilliant images attracted him; however they have also led him from difficulties everyone in Ireland must live with. He has allowed himself to be dominated by America or by countries in close nexus with her. To be avant-garde away from one of the main centers harbingers the creation of art which is passé from its moment of inception.

The poems gathered in *Anatomy of a Cliché* are somewhat successful attempts at expressing an identity not *bound* by Irish thought. In these poems, all of which resay the old cliché "I love you" in terms more exacting and evocative, Hartnett lets Ireland, as well as other countries important to him, be a referent for his self. In the eighth poem, the identification is made:

I will pay court to you
after an antique irish fashion. . . .[4]

He has a few other poems about Ireland, as well as ones relating to his understanding of the German, Greek, French, and Japanese experiences or understandings. As in this obviously Japanese one:

the snow is gone
the cherry trees
drop white petals
cold as snow
on my face.[5]

These poems, however, are not mononationalistic, but multinationalistic, resembling in this sense those of Pearse Hutchinson. Hartnett does not use, though, the conversational approach so favored by most of his peers.

*Leland*
*Bardwell*

Leland Bardwell expresses a sureness of artistic belief which intimates a personal security lacking in so much poetry similar and contemporary with hers. In "Leixlip and the Rye" she wrote of the meeting of the Leixlip with the Liffey with the enthusiasm of Anna Livia but without her complexity and incipient despair with reality:

> Where a lady ran guns in the troubles
> And other ladies cried
> Watching their Georgian Mansions crumble.[6]

Her readiness to view life as a mixture of the heroic and ridiculous, with small and beautiful lives, and man's destructiveness gives the poetry of Leland Bardwell a center that will enable her to treat subjects of traumatic involvement without the frenetic intensity of Anne Sexton and Sylvia Plath.

For whatever the reason, poetic tradition or personal resistance, Leland Bardwell has been able to turn the dangers and disappointments of modern sexual freedom into clever, but never anxiety-ridden, poetry. Perhaps, the example of Con Marckewitz, as well as the ladies of the gardens, gave her precedent for accepting destruction and for creating when one's form of life has atrophied or been obliterated. In her poems she has been able to accept the chance and instability of life. In "Sentimental Journey" she wrote of two couples on a holiday. One couple "clicked," and the other went through the emotions.[7] In "Lament" she writes of a woman who has lost a lover and finds that pride goes before a fall:

> And all my friends who are so nice
> Now bludgeon me with their advice
> "You do not need this Casanova
> When you can have me as a lover."
>
> So I cut again and cut the decks,
> (There is no substitute for sex)
> Alas, I can not save my face;
> I can not cut the God-damned ace![8]

Yeats's Crazy Jane had such honesty, as did many of the Cavalier poets. However, the tone and honesty are not part of the great tradition of poetry in English. Women, especially, are supposed to be more dedicated to a lover than are men, less motivated by the physical need for sexual love than men, or at least dedicated to seeming so. Leland Bardwell's baring the feminine mind with its machinations so similar to the masculine gives her the striking contemporaneity of Sylvia Plath, whom she resembles, without the frightening anguish and hostility. I doubt that Leland Bardwell could have written of the difference between men and women with such ferocity as Sylvia Plath makes the theme of "Lady Lazarus."[9] Both of these poetesses are personal, confessional in fact; however, Sylvia Plath's poetry examines human phenomena at its most frenetic level. Life of such danger becomes essential to art for her because, as Anne Sexton said, they were both "sucking" on death.[10] But Leland Bardwell stopped short of moving her personal observations into permanent psychological states. Instead, she expressed her involvements and disturbances through social states that are hardly reinforced by psychological generalizations. In "A Prayer for All Young Girls," for instance, Leland Bardwell does not go further than a description of the modern woman as she views her:

> Dear God, make me sophisticated,
> Dear God, make me highly equipped;
> Dear God, make me easily bored,
> Not tolerant, hard-working, energetic,
> Not sober nor militant.
> Dear God, make me rich, taxi-minded, expeditious,
> Vicious at the right times.
> Make me, dear God,
> A thorough-going sex-ridden bitch. Amen.[11]

Leland Bardwell does not look for other than the signs of the type, which may be a way of saying she is content with the surface or cannot turn from a sardonic view of the patina of woman.

Why such a different treatment of similar subjects should occur can, of course, be explained simply with the differences between the writers as human beings. But seen together, the contemporary Irish writers have been hesitant to accept the conclusions and methods of psychoanalysis as having so elemental an importance as have American writers. The writers of the time of Yeats and Joyce had their own mythology in which they had created the image of themselves they wanted. To accept Freud or Jung as makers of myths to replace the ones they had developed would be to reject the purpose of the myths: to create a self-conscious Irishness which would lead to respect and action. The internationalism of psychoanalysis would refocus attention. The younger generation found no merit in the mythic pose of Yeats and Joyce, though the latter through the common humanity of his characters remains favored. Though it may help some of the poets, analysis has generally been a means, not a subject. The culture of Ireland remains the most formidable structure of the Irish mind.

*James Liddy*

This mention of Joyce calls to mind a writer most illustrative of the idea of *Arena*, James Liddy. More than any contributor and more than Michael Hartnett and Michael Cane (the other two editors), James Liddy expressed the central ideas of the periodical. The idea from which all others came, Liddy described when he wrote that Joyce showed the catastrophe of European civilization and the phoniness of academia. (From its inception, *Arena* had rejected academic critics.) Love of humanity is the center of Joyce: "His love is the degree I took."[12] Such a view of Joyce is certainly a possible one and does form a meeting point for the basic theme of *Arena*: the continual avowal of love and sympathy for the mistreated and an attempt to update the culture of Ireland.

*Arena* had other ties with Irish culture than the expression of a view of humanity easily derived from Joyce. The avant-garde attitude appears to grow from an awareness of the changing state of the populace, as seen in Liddy's description of his own background: "My tradition: the professional classes at one remove from the rural farm. My patriotism: my great grandfather and great uncle were evicted in County Clare and were better Fenians than Yeats claimed to be. My father's family, though sadly Redmondite, had little sympathy for the landlord class from which they made their money. I was particularly imbued with distaste against those Catholics who supported the rule of the British Government in Ireland and took office under the Crown when this was conceded to them."[13] Such a progression is a typical one for the literate Irishman.

Much of the excitement of *Arena*, and the consequent irritation with it, results from the lack of a specific bias. The freedom of expression allowed by the editors often brought into print series of poems of interminable sameness, essays of irritating inaccuracy. But in all cases the writers tried to avoid the easy poses predicated by the past and the facile pose of rejection of that past. Again, it is James Liddy who wrote most pointedly about an obvious lack of honesty among the Dublin intelligentsia:

> *The Blind Bitter Town 1965*
> A centenary is an excuse for those revisionists who hate art (academics, journalists, publishers, failed poets, women out of love) to make themselves important. Yeats cannot rage at them, being but a book, yet surely two things would give him pleasure: the visit of Ezra Pound to see his wife and the return of Roger Casement. Putting a plaque on George Moore's house would amuse him.[14]

Being able to say Yeats is "but a book" represents a significant advance in the poetry of modern Ireland, which has been disregarded by critics and most other poets alike since the death of Yeats. But Liddy does not discard Yeats. Instead, he emulates his scorn for artificiality and admires his art. Probably nothing more is of importance, for the Anglo-Irish view of the world is passé. Only Robert Graves, whom the editors of *Arena* described as the "last of the Anglo-Irish poets," at all resembles those grand gesturers of the past.[15]

Liddy's refusal to conceal or deny the ordinariness of his ancestry indicates a very basic difference between him and his contemporaries, and Yeats. He constructed an idea of himself as Irish without invoking the precedent of the eighteenth century, without appealing to Swift, Goldsmith, and Berkeley. Knowing he has not their grandeur, nor their madness, in his blood, Liddy admits the commonness of his humanity:

> In a pub west of Shannon where they sell shrouds
> And the landlord's burnt house stands low on the hill
> I drank stout with farmers and read my fate.[16]

Liddy's easy musings on sex and his acceptance of ordinary farmers (so different from Yeats's peasants) would have been jarringly inconsistent for the writers of the Literary Revival.

In *Esau My Kingdom for a Drink* Liddy stressed the importance of James Joyce to his own culture. Joyce found in his love of common people an attitude he struck in each book he wrote, each with a definite didactic purpose:

> So you, James Joyce, loving us seriously all the time behind our backs like a father, caring for us as unmarried virgins who might die without kissing life, still walking our pavements from your books and showing us our hypocrisy and time-serving, you, comradeless, hoping as you wrote but telling none that we, in our green isle of only human snakes, should read your armoury of words and begin to live.[17]

Here is reiterated the editorial policy of love and sympathy for the common, for the unfortunate. This love is the indigenous quality of the Irish, at least of the best: "You, the greatest son of Catholic Ireland in seven hundred years, how many things you were to us, how near from our bogland you flew to the sun of truth of life, how like all of us you were searching for the father, Bloom-Shakespeare, hidden in the deep bones to which we long to return."[18]

Liddy's first volume of poetry, *In a Blue Smoke*, brings the readers into an awareness of the difference between the poet and the people to whom he had once been so close. "By the Western Seaboard" tells of life in the town where he once lived. There the people watch every season "an Abbey potboiler," which but interrupts briefly the silence of their lives, the inertia of their lives. Liddy asks:

> What has made me different (my mother sitting there on a stool, examined by a jury of six silent eyes) and yet the same, catching their digs on the rebound? O my people lost from words since the Education Act and the University Acts and that bit of American money![19]

The mention of American money is another tie to Liddy's past concerns, the dangers and inequities of life in America. As much as anything else, his awareness of the powers shaping life must separate him from his silent people.

Being separate from them, yet unwilling to accept the opposite extreme, America (though he has taught in America), which is "at the cross bombs of history and ideology," he turns to love, the ultimate worship, and European culture. Love is important in and constantly unites Liddy's work. It was his theme in *Arena* and in

*Esau My Kingdom for. . . .* In his first volume, a poem entitled "Anne" expands the matter:

> She runs to her own, in jeans and sweater to herself.
> Further than any adventure love waits to be told.
>
> Pure without mirrors and the light shining within.
> She sleeps on milk of the moon Our Lord and Our Lady.
>
> So holy, holy, holy is love, all love, my loving:
> I caress her upon my typewriter, I type her out.[20]

A muse wearing jeans and a sweater who is equated with the Virgin Mary seems to be consciously contrived to provide shock value. However, the poem does not shock. It delights with warmth and massing memories evoked of gentle days and women.

Consistently, Liddy resists the temptation to write beyond the object. Even in coining the term "Christ-sex" he is concerned with an example, not with a religious or psychological generalization. Christ gave all without bargaining for a guaranteed return before he would commit himself. His love is like theirs:

> Which says no to the sad bargain of trading
>          in the pure unpossessed
> For the usual slow-dying love; happy you sit
>          alone in thought giving.[21]

This poem is not a meek meditation on the example of Christ, but rather an explanation of why they will not marry and why "routine sex" has no appeal to them. As he combined traditional religious views with contemporary attitudes and actions, so he did in "Dear One, A Saint." Liddy has uncovered a viable third choice of muses for Irish poets who have traditionally been limited to the unseen and untouched beauty of legend or to the haus frau. He concurs with Desmond O'Grady: "Never marry your muse."[22]

In a poem "For Sean O'Casey" Liddy uses again his technique of basing a poem on a familiar sight, the meaning of which he has changed. The red star "on top of the Telefis Eireann mast" calls to his mind poor children he had seen playing, his fear of the police because they might put him in prison for not holding the traditional idea about the haves and the have-nots. He explains that he offers the children no bribe to follow his views:

> instead I give you the red star,
> his red star that is over Ballsbridge,
> to him and me the sign of a holy utopia:
> the revolution we imagine
> in which each of us will love
> the other one according to his need
> and the other will love us
> according to what is our need
> because in the end
> we were created equal and free.
> Yes, equal my children,
> free my children![23]

In the course of the poem the red star becomes identified with that of communism and with Christ's star. What else could "his star" be intended to connote? What role does that leave O'Casey to play? Again the associations are dangerously close to losing value by means of over-emphasized associations.

Liddy's refusal, or inability, to expand and modify the significance of his images by transforming them into metaphors does at times succeed. In his poems about the Jews killed during World War II, Liddy finds images which successfully arouse compassion and guilt, especially for the young and politically concerned Irishman. He reflects on a New Year's Eve service in Limerick:

> No public prayers for six million burnt-up Jews;
> remember we were pro German and wanted them to
> beat the English. . . .[24]

He recalls the same experience and emotions in "If Christ Walked Again: Beatitudes, 1960":

> Blessed are the Jews; and holy because of them our
> conscience is the never absent smells of the
> gas oven and crematorium.[25]

The effectiveness of these poems depends upon the enforcement of guilt by the whole of western civilization.

Liddy's poems for all of their "concreteness" rely on European associations. As was true with *Arena* in general, the most forceful of Liddy's poems are those which deal with clearly evident and emotionally charged cultural phenomena, such as racial discrimination. His concern with the effect of such memories and forces on his own being suggests the poetry of Sylvia Plath and others for whom confession is an important part of poetry. In "To the Memory of Sylvia Plath: A Personal Note," he pays respect to the dead poetess in her own mode:

Demon alcohol makes me tick before tea;
like the unmarried I try to liquify my longings. . . .[26]

Liddy differs from Plath in the range of his interests, his European consciousness, and in the lower intensity of his poems. Like many of his contemporaries, he looks to a new Europe for identification, perhaps hoping Ireland will become again an integral part of the European community.

Liddy is caught between the vibrant and excited experience of membership in a new internationalism and the appeal of a graceful past. Such a man as Bernard Berenson represents this past:

such a head
shall not bite again the four corners
of our European dust and glory.[27]

Liddy describes Berenson surrounded by his memories and the beauty he had collected, using all to "wanding off progress like Prospero." For Liddy, Berenson is a beautiful memory of a time so much more graceful than today. No mention is made of Berenson's being Jewish and American, of his suffering indignities, of his being used by the business community, of his quietly and delicately adopting a civilized ethic. Liddy used the memory of Berenson as he says Berenson used his memories, as protection in a time of bluntness and even crassness. How can one be otherwise when the modern world has expunged gentleness and taste with the same frenetic drive that Hitler tried to rid the world of Jews.

*Arena* lived without regard for exactness of fact and typography, which angered people for whom a magazine is judged only by its regularity and correctness in both. However, *Arena* lived with flair. Its editors and contributors cavorted, were reputed to run the periodical from McDaid's, refused to take life seriously. Much of this was true. But they did take seriously the quality of material they published; and without the precarious excitement surrounding *Arena*, many of the works published would have received less notice at their first appearance. Montague believes "The Seige of Mullingar" would not have been as immediately important if published in a less flamboyant organ.[28] Understanding the enthusiasm of *Arena*, then, we must accept its begrudging death, its momentary burst into life again, and the departure of some of its editors to exotic lands.

For two issues *Arena* returned under the title *The Holy Door*. Printed in stencil on legal-size sheets of paper with poor control over typography and facts, *The Holy Door* outshone its parent, though only slightly. In the first issue, Brian Lynch, editor, explained the purpose of *The Holy Door*:

> This magazine will be devoted to 'Looking around' for life; devoted to the new mind and the new eye — glimpses of which were to be found in *Arena*. . . .This magazine hopes to find and encourage the passion of eye and intelligence; hopes to find another country, hopes to make it new for Ezra Pound. Adjust the eyescrew.[29]

The invocation of Pound seems out of place at first for the blessing of a liberal magazine. But consider that Pound, like the editors of *Arena* and *The Holy Door*, had his complaint with the capitalist establishment; and he too believed in the power of art to change the course of history. That Pound has taught most of the poets in this century how to write cannot be overlooked.

The list of contributors in the first issue sparkled, but unexpectedly: James Liddy, Thomas Kinsella, Desmond O'Grady, Leland Bardwell, Michael Hartnett, Tony Cronin, Christie Brown. Cronin provided a long poem, "Character," which summarizes the iconoclastic temper of *The Holy Door* and at the same time reflects back to the discouragement and cynicism which must have set in after the end of *Envoy*. So much bad has happened in the world that seemed good once. By 1965, even those departing realized that Ireland and nationality were not to be avoided. The poem must, as Auden once wrote, record the history.

Leland Bardwell has her own well-established flair as one of the free people of Dublin, and her poem, "Childhood Reminder," in the first issue of *The Holy Door* has the precedent of her earlier modern love poems:

> There is no romance for me
> In the graveyard crowded with bones
> Only in a room crowded with vulgar people
> With my lover at the other end.[30]

Her welcoming of the new, unsophisticated (perhaps crude) life of Dublin complements well Cronin's reflections on his past, which wanted to open the door into a literature different from that of the puritanical and romanticizing past.

But past and present come together frequently in a poem, "Brendan," by Christie Brown. Only recently the literary world outside Ireland has been surprised by the ability of this paralyzed man. His novel, *Down All the Days*, has been widely acclaimed. In the first issue of *The Holy Door*, his talent was already there to be seen as with an unexpected joy he gives a self-portrait, "myself blissfully plastered in the wheelchair," before describing Brendan Behan, a wild Irish writer who has become an emblem of iconoclasm for the present generation:

> He was all my Saturday nights rolled into one,
>     the harlequin
>         of every hooley, the wonder of every wake,
>             the terror of the fair state, observed of all
>                 observers,
>                     spanner in the works of insidious deceit,
> a shaggy-headed Pan with a song for the ugly,
>     the maimed,
>         the unclaimed,
>             a crowned and drowned King Puck clowning
>                 for the populace,
>                     ribbing the lean ribs of the rigid righteous
> with his Rabelaisian panacea of ribald rhetoric
>     anointing our wounds with salt of his soul.[31]

This poem may well prove to be the most exceptional piece in either *Arena* or *The Holy Door* and not because of the difficulty with which it had to be composed. Christie Brown understands so well what being an outsider means that he saw with clarity the solitary, destructive life of Behan. Basic to all of the new literature is the understanding that permanence, like an ontological deity, may not again for a long time inform a whole society.

The second, and final, issue of *The Holy Door* added Auden, Montague, Hutchinson, and Milne to several from the first. Generally, the writing concerns Ireland as a modern, not antique, country with subjects taken from the neurotic, deviant, passionate world of people. John Montague, in his self-reflecting way, takes the reader into every childhood in "Return," as he himself journeys into memory:

> Seeing your former
> self saunter up the garden path
> afterwards, would you flinch,
> acknowledging that sensuality,
> that innocence?[32]

To remind the Irish of their own humanity has largely motivated the writer today. In this poem, seemingly so mild, the shock of a sensual child figures significantly. That a wide audience will hear or receive such knowledge is doubtful; nevertheless, the need remains.

### CHAPTER IV

# Poetry Ireland and Irish Writing

These two periodicals suggest the coming maturity of Irish poetry. The time period, from 1946 (when *Irish Writing* began) to 1968 (when the new *Poetry Ireland* ended), covers the most important battles between the internationalists and the living tradition of the dead giants of the Literary Revival. No one still involved with the identity of the Irish writer could avoid the conflict.

*Irish Writing* and *Poetry Ireland* stated their concern in quite similar terms. The foreward to the first issue of *Irish Writing* stresses that the poets are at a crossroad:

> Our poets are many. At the moment, perhaps, they are sulking a little overcome by the shadow of Ben Bulben. But this is an *ombrage* which at least they share with most of the English-speaking world. And signs there are that other talents, poets of the young and vigorous, are advancing into the sunlight.[1]

Attention is also called to the "abounding variety" of poetry in contemporary Ireland. P. J. Madden in *Irish Writing* also rejected an "Irish mode" of writing which would limit the theme and subject of writing in Ireland to traditional music, and language. He did not, however, posit the contrary, a completely un-Irish internationalism, but called for tolerance and freedom.[2] Though this concern for the new and a desire to avoid the old ways motivates these two periodicals, both enter the conflict — though without the singularity of purpose that *Envoy* did.

Unquestionably, the approach of *Poetry Ireland* was partially determined by the presence of writers for *Envoy*, now defunct. Iremonger and Cronin published poetry in the new periodical, though neither seemed determined to begin another battle. In fact, Cronin published two poems on distinctly Irish subjects. "On An Old Story" recalls a bloody and violent act from ancient Ireland:

> To take her from his arms, I too,
> had I been Conor,
> Would have twisted my mouth in treachery,
> abandoned honor.[3]

Much in the way of the internationalists, Cronin concerns his poem with the psychological similarity of people, regardless of time and place. In a later poem, "Consolation," though, he writes of the contemporary poets' desire for traditional rewards and reflects on the problems caused by a lack of money and the lack of recognition as the same experienced by the wandering Gaelic poets:

> And wanting a firelit hall
> And a prince's head to be bowed
> In acquiescence to the word. . . .[4]

This memory within poets of their traditional importance to ancient Ireland may well exist for many, but seldom becomes so openly stated. Cronin's form and contemporary concern with the problems of poets keep his poem from being simply a nostalgic period piece.

Kavanagh, however, became even more fervent and found praise for his ability continuing. In the first issue of *Poetry Ireland*, Kavanagh is attributed, probably by David Marcus, with emblematic significance for contemporary Ireland:

> A poet who keeps his eye firmly on some object in the distance and proceeds towards it with the purpose and high seriousness that characterize Kavanagh's work will, sooner or later, halt momentarily to issue some statement more important, more considerable, than the sum of his previous poems.[5]

Within ten years, Kavanagh is to find that his "purpose is to have no purpose," thus calling into question such an eloquent tribute as the one above. But in the late forties, even in the early fifties, Kavanagh was a rallying point for many who would strike a new note, an un-Yeatsian note. In 1947 Kavanagh replied to a comment about his censure of Higgins in terms that would have excited any of the young internationalists. To clarify whether he censured the dead F. R. Higgins as a writer of bad verse or as a writer of Protestant verse, Kavanagh wrote:

> NOTE: The editors suggest that my thesis gives the impression that I think a Protestant cannot be an Irish writer, and have asked if I would disclaim such a theory.
>
> My immediate reaction would be: Who wants to be an Irish writer! A man is what he is, and if there is some mystical quality in the Nation or the race it will ooze through his skin. Many Protestants, doubting that their Irishism would ooze, have put it on from the outside. National characteristics are superficial qualities and are not the stuff with which the poet deals. The subject matter of the poet is the universal and in this he is one with Catholicism.[6]

That Protestants can have authentic local coloration is proved by such names as Standish O'Grady, Dunsany, O'Casey. But they didn't consciously desire this.[7] His rejection of Higgins, then, is of a man who adopted "coloration" in an attempt to become part of a culture. The censure may well be justified.

*Ewart Milne*

The attempt of the Protestant community to accept the value of Kavanagh is illustrated by Ewart Milne's evaluation. After first describing himself as Protestant and proclaiming the political importance of the "Protestant 'individual choice' and its 'freedom of choice'" as being more of a deterrent to Communism than is possible for Catholicism to be, Milne continues:

> At the same time, your national poet must be truly the most representative poet of his people, of all or at least the majority of his countrymen. In this sense I think Patrick Kavanagh is nearer to being our national poet than Yeats.[8]

In a letter Milne spoke of the importance of Kavanagh at this time in very similar terms. Kavanagh represented a tradition opposite to Yeats's and seemed very much "the ploughboy poet."[9]

Milne's own background is Anglo-Irish, though he was in self-exile for twenty-five years from Ireland. After he remarried and returned to Ireland with his new wife, he began writing for *Poetry Ireland* and *Irish Writing*. Though his poetry had consistently dealt with Irish themes, especially Yeatsian, he now seemed very much concerned with reestablishing his identity within the literary community.

Milne has been a literary outsider who often made discoveries in style and thought before they became *au courant* and then moved on to other ways before he had fully assimilated his own work. He early, and perhaps late, viewed the Ireland in which he lived, the Ireland of past poets, as one which encouraged the cultivation of basic truths. However, these truths impose limitations on man that, for good or bad, are intolerable. His rejection of an inherited ethic is the theme of the early volume *Listen Mangan*. In "Poem for Wet Weather" he describes, extensively, the Ireland with which he is "sick." The poem is a despairing one; for in fact Milne has grown sick of the "earth" and only uses Ireland with "its stones, its cliffs, its beaches, its fields, its houses and god-boxes . . . its tragic history, its starving people, its intolerable secrecy" as the occasion for his disgust and disillusionment.[10] Like all the contemporary poets in Ireland I have mentioned he desires freedom from a great but debilitating literary past. He would forget O'Flaherty, O'Connor, Shaw, Swift, Lever, Edgeworth, Somerville and Ross — all past writers held up as measures of present worth. His advice to people living in the present is, "Come let us pray for the modern Irish novel."[11] He rejects causes that destroy or reduce to insignificance human individuality, the continued growth of man. Though Milne's politics until recently were quite left of center, he censured even the labor movement of James Connolly. Connolly had wanted the "Earth" for his workers: "Now Hitler is wanting the earth for Germans."[12] The parallel shocks, but illuminates Milne as a free and perhaps anarchic spirit.

Milne's action and ideas are not determined by attachment to abstract principles. A specific and personal involvement precedes his expression of sympathy with an ideology. For instance, he enlisted in the Medical Aid Corps in the Spanish Civil War for quite personal, as well as political, reasons. A man of such liberal beliefs that his own conservative father banished him from home, also, would be attracted to the Loyalists. But essentially he went to the war because of friendship for a man. The man believed very strongly in the political struggle. When he was killed, Milne's own interest waned. The off-handed and impersonal way comrades in arms reacted to his friend's death repulsed him.[13] At his best Milne is a poet who recognizes only the need for love and respect. No amount of unpleasantness seems able to do more than mitigate his openness and wonder. The late poem, *Time Stopped*, well proves his commitment to joy even when distressed by human weakness and wrong.

He has long been impressed with Joyce, another literary and actual exile. He suggests a kinship with Joyce's view of man as Irishman in "Chamber Music":

I speak these words to the sea that is rising:
I say his greatness mirrored our sickness,
    our evasion,
Is it by sickness and evasion you would honor him?[14]

In a letter Milne explained the circumstances of this poem's publication: "I wrote 'Chamber Music' when Joyce died in January 1941, the great editor of *The Irish Times*, R. M. Smyllie, took it for publication with the remark that most people in Ireland only knew Joyce as the author of a dirty book, a scandalous figure, but he would publish it just the same. It was years after before Dublin discovered that Joyce was an Industry, and every student got on the bandwagon with a Joyce thesis."[15] The poem and the comment reveal much about Milne's relationship to Ireland and Joyce. He acts as an offspring who loves but must reject his parents. The squabbles between Joyce and his country obviously distressed Milne, who finds himself caught in the middle — bound to both. His answer to the dilemma of choosing between them is a self-exile resembling Joyce's but more thorough. And the ethic he postulates has often been made by his contemporaries, though Milne cites Auden in making his: "We must love one another or die."[16] He did not believe such love could become an important theme in his work and principle in his life if he continued to live in Ireland. He left Ireland, accepting Smyllie's comment that to do so would banish him from the minds of his countrymen.[17]

The influence of Joyce is not as obvious as that of Yeats in the early poems of Milne, but it is there. In *Galion* the title character is an abstraction of the mock-hero of *Ulysses*: "Then Galion cut an ashplant stick from a hazel wood Crying Excelsior, my trusty sword."[18] The poems continue in this sardonic way to castigate Ireland. Milne, in his early poetry, fits this tone to his many allusions to Yeats. Just as for the writers of *Envoy*, for Milne Yeats is the enemy. In "Channel Spray" he alludes to "Parnell" and "The Old Stone Cross," which has for its refrain, "Said the man in the golden breastplate/Under the old stone Cross"[19]:

> What do they make of Ireland,
> Of Fianna girls and Fianna boys?
> De Valera, Lemass, and Boland,
> What do they make of Ireland?
> *Said the man in the militia jacket*
> *That he got in the war in Spain.*[20]

Whereas Yeats's poem is an ecstatic prediction of the continuation of man and the return of the aristocrat-hero, Milne reverses the view by making his poem an ironic comment on destruction which Yeats ignored. Death and war affected both men in much the same way; but for Milne, Yeats represented a view of life which encourages such violence. Milne sardonically rejects the epics to which Yeats always returned, as he indicated in "Water for the Rose," a poem about his rejection of a prescribed ideology:

> The traveller lost in them is found —
> said I to Yeats' ghost
> whose sickles make the sword to yield,
> whose hammers ring from coast to coast —
> so get you gone, there's life to build!
> said I to Yeats' ghost.[21]

Much of Milne's objection to Yeats was caused by their differing political beliefs at the time: Yeats so conservative and Milne so liberal. Milne's own views have changed; and he now believes Yeats to have been right, himself to have been wrong. In his rewriting of this poem, the stanza quoted above is to be omitted.[22] The poem will end with Yeats's ghost saying:

Be Lenin's host or whose you will,
The stubborn ghost replied;
Mate the birch-tree with the rowan,
the rose take for the sunflower's bride;
the lost traveller and the hill
will wait on your rejoicings still.[23]

Part of Milne's reason for the change is that he has come to believe in his own talent as an essentially romantic and lyrical one, not ironic and strongly political.

Though he has changed many of his political and poetic beliefs, the poems he wrote earlier accurately exemplify much that was important to him and to Ireland when he wrote them. In "The Fool of the World" Milne again modified a poem by Yeats to explain his own relationship to the past:

Who knows, he'll cease his roguery, tire of ruin,
Marry the matron, and leave the slip of a moon alone.
Who knows, his allegorical sire and dam —
The stallion of Eternity, and the great mare of Time,
In disgust will banish him. But will they breed again?
*I'll breed said his sire Eternity. But not on me said the mare of Time.*[24]

Even in this rejection of Yeats's poem, "Tom At Cruachan," Milne reveals a concern with his literary past and an acceptance of Yeats's poetic power.[25] Milne, like Eliot, seems to use the verse form itself as a comment upon his time and the time in which the form he uses occurred. The use of Yeats's favorite ballad form is ironic and limited. The title poem of his first volume of selected verse, *Diamond Cut Diamond*, is quite similar to what we have come to call "concrete poetry," though his precedent would be the shaped verse of the Renaissance:

Two cats
One up a tree
One under the tree
The cat up the tree is he
The cat under the tree is she
The tree is witch elm, just incidentally.
He takes no notice of she, she takes no notice of he.

> He stares at the woolly clouds passing, she stares at the tree
> There's been a lot written about cats, by old Possum, Yeats, and
>            Company,
> But not Alfred de Musset or Lord Tennyson or Poe or anybody
>      Wrote about one cat under, and one cat up a tree.
>            God knows why this should be left for me
>                 Except I like cats as cats be
>                   Especially one cat up
>                   And one cat under
>                       A witch elm
>                         Tree.[26]

This poem represents what Milne does so well: the light, sardonic verse of Eliot in *Old Possum's Book of Practical Cats* or of Ogden Nash. But Milne's concern is different from theirs in that he is more serious. This was the first poem he published in *Poetry Ireland* and has about it the air of a pronouncement, albeit a seemingly casual one.

Milne's publishing in *Poetry Ireland* and *Irish Writing* was not a long one, lasting only until 1951, but he published regularly until then.[27] Though protesting about the state of Ireland, he did not deny his tie to the country; and these two periodicals seriously attempted to create a new and healthy literary life. Like many of his contemporaries, Milne desired clarity in his poems. Unlike most of them, he also desired lyricism. In his light poems, his concern to be accepted as himself, as in "Cri De Nos Temps," is a reply to the complaint that poetry is not what it used to be. For Milne, this complaint masks a fear:

> Lest a poem one day
> Might be so clear
> It would explode in your ear:
> Then where would you be? But where![28]

Quite frequently, nostalgia for a quieter age combined with bitterness towards an age which has been inherited and denied the grace and beneficence of the past creates a mood of despair in the midst of ugliness. The reaction is quite human. But in "Against Epitaphs," family and ancient traditions of beauty and peace have all been replaced by crews of workmen who clear away the rubble of war.[29]

In *Once More to Tourney*, Milne's next volume, the themes are much more despairing and bitter. "Johnny Crusoe" is about a man who lived in the South Seas with six wives. There, "He begat, and swore, and lived outside." After describing the gusto and joy of this old style hero, Milne contrasts his own time with that of Crusoe:

P.S. Johnny Crusoe was not long dead
When the H-bombs went off above his head,
And now with him his children lie
And poisoned rolls the coral sea. . . .[30]

The assessment of the present as small and mean typified much of the writing of the thirties, a time with which Milne associates himself. The sardonic levity with which Milne approaches his own time has at least three obvious causes: the dilemma of the contemporary Anglo-Irishman who is more between the stools than ever, explained in "Family Drinking Song" and "Little Boy Delinquent"; the continuing influence of the unconverted Eliot, as in "Cockles and Mussels"; and the post-war despairing of ever again finding a more than transitory joy, as in "The Girl in the Train."[31] Milne reflects in his poetry the widespread inability, or refusal, of contemporary man to extend the significance of an experience beyond the experience. No social or cultural metaphor exists to justify or stabilize an experience. Man can only understand and explain what happens to him and what he does. Nothing is repeated with great enough regularity and completeness for him to develop norms based upon actual experiences. Milne's most recent, and most unsettling, treatment of this subject is *Time Stopped*, a long poem interspersed with prose.[32] Milne attempts to understand his life after the death of his wife and to reconcile himself to a betrayal he learned about after her death. Again, his poetry can be seen in terms of a major "school" of contemporary poetry: the confessional. The psyche is bared, and the poet's trauma and distress become the end rather than the means of poetry. Milne has not taken for his own readily available poetic styles. As J. M. Cohen observed, he has a voice of his own and has not given in to fads and styles.[33] Milne's variations on themes and approaches taken by Lowell, Plath, MacBeth are, perhaps, best explained by his ancestry and nation. Being Anglo-Irish he was at birth separated from the bulk of the people in his nation. Being Irish and a writer he expects to be rejected by his reading public as were Yeats, Synge, Joyce, and O'Casey. In "Happy as Larry — And He Stretched" Milne uses an in-joke (Donagh MacDonagh wrote a play *Happy as Larry* about a wake) as an ironic comment upon the death of a contemporary poet:

> 'Tis the like is the ruin of Ireland,
> With their heathenish loves and communist ways,
> Bad luck to them all, by the Holy!
> And worse luck to this fella we've buried today —
> May he corner no corner in history!
> *He has? Well, if that isn't a mystery!*[34]

This poem contains much of the Dublin view of Ewart Milne, a man who is known to write "very fierce letters to the newspapers."[35] But of more importance in this poem is his sardonic attack on the viciousness that characterizes the Irish literary world, both in terms of the writers themselves and the reading public's reaction to the writers.

In *Time Stopped*, Ewart Milne entered a literary, and personal, war with more vengeance than anyone in modern times. Joyce might attack, but never without shaping the experience. But Milne was angered beyond all tolerance by a friend's betrayal. After his wife's death, he discovered she had been intimately involved with a very close friend of his, who was also married. In the poem, Milne attacks not his wife, but the other couple, whom he accused of maliciously bilking the Milnes. All of the poem is confessional; and much of it is a Freudian-based analysis of his marriage:

> And in your wildness the con-man saw his chance
> Perhaps he seemed a younger me to you
> As your daughter was a younger you to me[36]

This vindication of his life and love with his wife coupled with the continual attack on G, the betrayer, creates a psychologically complex statement.

Milne returns to an earlier ethic. Though he makes frequent reference to his liberal politics, at one point he assumes a mask that comes from Ireland's, if not Milne's, Anglo-Irish past:

If this had been in duelling days
And if he had been one fit for me to call out
    Since only between equals in honour's rank
      Was duelling possible at all
Then I would have slapped my glove across his face
He would have had to challenge me or be shamed
I would have had choice of weapons sword or gun.[37]

Milne in his days as a wandering sailor or an aide in Spain may have tried to abandon his heritage, largely because the father could not accept the son's liberal politics.[38] Always he returned and increasingly accepted his identity, perhaps coming to find value in an idea of self that has the stability of precedent and practice:

I exist in an un-Celtic twilight not alive and not dead
In the Lethe of invisible poets in the semi-shade
Yet I take pride in being of the Anglo-Irish breed
Of those more Irish than the Irish in the old days[39]

Though Milne had early rejected the language and always the traditional sagas, he came at last to need a heritage, one based on, of all things, Ireland. Reflecting back over the difficulties and problems that Milne has dealt with prepares for this conclusion. Though he has struggled to be free of the "nets" of nation, ancestry, and religion, Milne remains as uncomfortably bound by them as was Joyce.[40] Also, unlike Joyce, Milne did not allow his ego to reduce the works and lives of others to insignificance. His admiration for the poetry of Yeats brings him to a tolerance of the man which complicates separation. In "Oboe for Yeats" Milne's drawing of a distinction is blurred by his reaction to the poetry itself:

Obliquely a hawk
skimmed low down the street
between pigeon houses.
My room window and I

reflected astonishment!
Yet when planes wall the sky
a hawk may be
a marvel, obliquely.
May be most marvelously
a hawk, not only the hawk of the mind.
The thing, itself, implicitly.[41]

Implicit in Milne's astonishment is praise of Yeats at the expense of lesser beings (those who live in "pigeon houses"). Especially in a time of the machine, this intruder from the wild is to be marvelled at. So, too, is Yeats a foreign and admirable being.

Milne found in these two periodicals a vital concern with Ireland as serious as his own. The wars, however, took their toll. Neither past nor present could be forgotten. It may well seem that the events Milne began recording in *Time Stopped* in 1964 caused his disaffection with Ireland, whereas they only seem to have made his exile more necessary. In the first issue of the revived *Poetry Ireland*, Milne published a poem that suggests Ireland is once again beginning to constrict him, to limit him with old labels and call up again old pains:

The Anglo-Irish Protestant breed are fading out now,
And so much the better, their enemies vow as they crow. . . .
I, however, think so too, and should know
Being of the breed myself (half redskin, half white man)
Such as both native Irish and true-blue English spurn.
So, neither my family tree nor where I live greatly matter,
And Irishness is but the green chaff we fist up and scatter.[42]

In time, Milne would have been forced to find his own place of removal from a tradition that repeatedly cast him out. Just as surely, he would again have to return, if only in a token sense. He has begun to do reviews again for *The Irish Press*, renewing perhaps a friendship with David Marcus who now edits a poetry page in the same newspaper.[43]

Milne considers himself to be of the same literary background and generation as Samuel Beckett, who also published in the first series of *Poetry Ireland* and in *Irish Writing*.[44] "Three

Poems" has a surprisingly Irish sound to it, especially for such an international writer as Beckett:

> I would like my love to die
> and the rain to be falling on the graveyard
> and on me walking the streets
> mourning the first and last to love me.

Beckett published also "Extract From Watt," indicating the seriousness of the efforts of David Marcus and his staff.[45] Though Beckett did not become "famous" until *Godot* cast him into the midst of the existential colony, he had effectively severed relations with Ireland before World War II, and the movement in all of his writing had been away from scenes and characters that have a distinctly English or Irish mark, such as *Murphy*. For Beckett to publish in these two periodicals added much to the quality they began with and continued to express. Few contemporary Irish writers of any real significance did not publish something. The writings of Dunsany, O'Faolain, MacNeice, Colum, Kavanagh provided the journals with the excitement of significant writers already well-recognized in the international literary world. These Irish writers through their publications proved the literature of their time and their culture contained values worth the attention of anyone. That many of these writers grew from the ethos of the Irish Literary Revival prepared their audience for a favorable reception since the attitudes and themes of their writing were familiar and well accepted.

*Denis*
*Devlin*

*Poetry Ireland* and *Irish Writing* were not limited to published writers of established reputation in the popular market. One of the writers who had long been recognized as important, though not popular, was Denis Devlin. In 1949 he published part of his long poem "The Heavenly Foreigner" in *Irish Writing*, and the following year *Poetry Ireland* had an issue devoted to the poetry of Devlin, a considerable recognition of his ability.[46] Though Devlin had published widely and won the approval of several important taste makers, including Allan Tate and Robert Penn Warren, he had been omitted from significance by Austin Clarke in *Poetry in Modern Ireland*.[47] Clarke seemed irritated by

Devlin's similarity to the "intellectual" poets of the Continent.[48] Understandably, David Marcus as one of the main editors of the new literature of Ireland would disagree. He did in commenting that Clarke's book became thinner as it approached the present.[49]

For Marcus to give such strong approval as he did to the poetry of Devlin indicates his desire to publish the best writing done by the contemporary writers. Like many of his contemporaries, Devlin worked to free his ability from the strictures of the Church and to find within the people of his country traces of the beauty and belief that have been celebrated by poets for hundreds of years. The effect of writers on the Continent made Devlin a European writer more than any of his contemporaries, though many held that as desirable. Also, Devlin's own progression was from a surrealistic portrayal of disgust to a mythic celebration of love. In his presentation of a psychological reality, metaphor becomes reality — separating him distinctly from the writers who grew into maturity during the time of *Envoy* and the early days of *Poetry Ireland*. His way was not to attack Church and State, as did Clarke and Kavanagh. Instead he searched within himself and those he loved for values and forms which could control the power of the community by making the individual part of an eternal and universal belief.

Seemingly every Irish writer must struggle with the demands of a church-trained conscience. Devlin's early poems are illustrative:

> Stinkarum, stankarum, buck,
> The old Scholastics say
> That the body is filth and muck
> and will be dust one day.[50]

This light and ironic ballad stanza, with others, gives the expected conclusion to the body of the poem: the tempted joy of love and the conditioned rejection of it. If one metaphor, theme, occurs most frequently in Devlin's first two volumes it is, in various forms, death-decay:

> The most important variant of this is the vulture:

> And round the waste of waters and the skies
> Only the carrion flap with whuling cries.[51]

This bird becomes more than his familiar; it becomes his understanding of his place in his culture, the single sign of his being. As Magdalen had her "sorrow of salvation," Orpheus his of loss, Deirdre hers of ecstasy and even the beasts of stolen offspring, he too has his sorrow. But his is of a different order:

> O paltry melancholy,
> dragging a songless boredom through sunless and stormless
>     days
> images firing his brain of never accomplished tasks
> disarming smile of humility hiding coward delays
> on tiptoe in dreams beside action, sophister strutting in
>     masks. . . .[52]

This poem, too, debates a course of action, a way of life; and the alternatives are always the same: life or despair.

Even these early poems suggest the mythic development of Devlin, especially when one considers the vulture as does Erich Neumann in an essay about Freud's understanding Leonardo's *St. Anne with Virgin and Christ Child*. In it is a vulture shape Freud saw as a sign of breast and penis, i.e., homosexuality. Neumann questions the conclusion, substituting that of the primordial self-fecundating Great Mother. By association the figure represents the Church.[53] That Devlin may have intentionally used Freud's interpretation is not really relevant, but Devlin's use of the bird as a symbol of death-corruption is.

In "Now" Devlin increased the probable equation between death and the Great Mother:

> And Pallas' bird, fixed in sepia sky
> Moveless as marble, spreads her iris wings.
> Patient and proud mirroring of reality;
> Arrogant gathering of sense and movement and passion
> To interpret to men the profoundest souls of a man
> Disgust and tire like a long drawn-out farewell. . . .[54]

He assesses, and rejects, the culture that has produced him. The central image of the first section contains both image and value. "Death and Her Beasts, Ignoble Beasts" repeats the vulture theme, identifying goddess with bird, the mirror-image of life that

depresses.[55] And "Communication from the Eiffel Tower" repeats his conscious identification of woman as a surrealistic metaphor of earth, life, itself: "Woman slapped up of ooze, not were
you a red angel would/ The dreaming whips of your arms into
earth absorb me."[56]

Devlin's ambivalence about the feminine power clearly
exists, for woman is the Church and also a desirable physical
being. But more basic is his view that the feminine is an all-
powerful deity which the male must reject or be destroyed by.
The sources of this view, though ideology may be a better term,
are two obvious ones: The Church which he has shown as turning
man away from the world (equivalent to the feminine) and the
example of Eliot. Eliot's mingling of realistic details in an unexpected manner is the basic technique of surrealists. And the
rejection of the world so important in Eliot's poetry, though not
his plays, is reflected in Devlin's "Liffey Bridge":

> In limp doorways
> They try out their heaven
> They grind at love
> With gritted kisses
> Then eyes re-opened
> Behold slack flesh
> Such an assassin
> Such a world![57]

Though every dark doorway in every somewhat seedy part of any
city offers such a scene, that this one is set by the Liffey calls to
mind Joyce's Anna Livia, the archetypal mother providing life.
Even without the added significance given by Joyce's Liffey, the
mythic force is present in the equations drawn between the
people in the doorways, heaven, and the world.

The poems in Devlin's next volume, *Lough Derg*, retain the
mythic structure and allusions, but do so ecstatically. Except for
occasional sardonic comments upon the ways of the wealthy,
diplomats, and others intricately involved in the workings of
socio-economic man, Devlin's remaining poems present the
ecstasy of man. He is no longer consumed with loathing for the
workings of the Church. In the title poem of the volume, he

recounts the yearly pilgrimage to the lake. Though he differs from the people around him by the fact of his awareness, he does in his own terms achieve their joy and humility before the divine: "All is simple and symbol in their world,/The incomprehended rendered fabulous."[58] While the people around him kneel to their God, the poet's mind celebrates a union of soul and body that allows the animal appetite to feed the spirit and gives as example druids and Christ of the Renaissance painters. He retains his censure of belief that destroys the physical:

> O earthly paradise!
> Hell is to know our natural empire used
> Wrong, by mind's moulting, brute divinities.[59]

The poetry becomes a religiously eclectic celebration of loved life.

The importance of Jansenism, with its denial of free will and assertion of man's corruption, may well make a discussion of Irish Catholicism difficult to speak of in such a term as orthodox. Devlin's inability to accept the Church's dictums is apparent in "Jansenist Journey" and is flatly stated in "West Pier": "Aboriginal anger and Christian terror/Wound happiness."[60] He constructs a belief combining the pagan goddess with the Christian worship of the separate soul. Understandably, Samothrace (where paganism and Christianity briefly merged) attracts his attention. In a poem about the Winged Victory of Samothrace, he wrote ecstatically of birth, copulation, and death:

> Our Lady of Victory!
>
> And your voice, which has the opulent contentment of a June stream, babbles
> And I feel with relief:
> Better in danger with the goddess than float like a barge on the sea:
>
> Fingers again at my throat
> Baptism by immersion in the numerous sea
> As the water closes over me, I see
> The impersonal gleam in your eyes
> And the lax ebb and flow of your breasts.[61]

55

Often, Devlin was to celebrate the goddess and describe her effect on all who saw her.

The heady ecstasy of many poems in *Lough Derg*, "Welcome My World," for example, becomes quieter in the last poems.[62] In these Devlin reveals his conquest of Jansenist morbidity through his acceptance of life, love, and death as each being valuable for its own sake. He is not the young man for whom life is seen as the reflection of death. Instead, Devlin writes from his understanding of joy, his expectation of death.

"The Colours of Love," which Devlin wrote to his wife Caren, contains his basic understanding of woman's effect on man:

> The crackling lightwaves overhead
> minimize our human year.
> O blond haunches! O white bed!
> O harmless, ultramundane fear![63]

She leads man to a celebration of existence more fundamental than his rationality can comprehend.

"The Heavenly Foreigner" is Devlin's ultimate celebration of the life and reality he has accepted.[64] Man in his structuring of ethical systems strives to protect himself from the non-rational joy that woman would lead him to:

> Rodents in the corn like the black gas in the heart of the sun
> The chase and the loving under the damp ditch
> Her blond laughter now indecent, her sexual
> Ascetic face with the bones loosened
>
> The first rejection is the first injustice
> And inadmissable then the crisp, indifferent blow
> By turn; the flesh gone fire and bones gone wood
> The brain stutters and stops.[65]

Life and destruction still exist separately for Devlin. They are contraries which mingle with interdependence. The ascetic and the sexual do not struggle to destroy one another, and life becomes sacred. To achieve this understanding, however, Devlin sacrificed much that the Judeo-Christian tradition had led him to believe, much about the dominance of the male, much about the nature of the divine.

Devlin's knowledge came from his surrender of a world structured on patriarchal bases and his acceptance of a belief that existed:

> Before that Eldest Son
> Had heard of the Princess,
> Before the Flood
> Had washed the world's kidneys. . . .[66]

To accept that early belief involves him in the ancient ritual of the male's worship of the goddess, of the male's adoration of the feminine, of the male's death and rebirth. His acceptance comes "when the foreign power intervened and made all the difference."[67] Devlin never describes, or even circumscribes, this power; but lets the reader come to understand it in the context of the poem as an ancient role of man within the matriarchy. Once the man becomes aware of this role, he and his woman are forever cast in a primordial and magical existence. Love has brought him to the ancient ritual of the year, the periodic sacrifice of the male to the prolific figure of woman. This return to nature worship in which his culturally conditioned memory recedes before this awareness of the union of man and nature leads the poet to reject his culturally conditioned memory. Although Devlin's references to ancient culture are to the Greek, the similarity between the way of life he writes about and the Celtic is notable. Both are "traditional" as Mircea Eliade uses the term. In such a society, human beings understand themselves as partaking in the archetypal, not the unique. Called to mind, of course, is Robert Graves, another Irish writer who succeeded in establishing a European identity. Interestingly, neither was actively involved in the literary wars.[68]

The central figure in the traditional society was the woman. This importance has existed for Devlin since his early poems in which he portrayed her with Eliotesque repugnance as the carrion consuming vulture. In "The Heavenly Foreigner" the woman is no longer the source of corruption, but of ecstatic understanding. Again for Devlin, she is an ontological, rather than literal figure:

How she stood, hypothetical-eyed and metaphor-breasted
Weaving my vision out of my sight
Out of my sight, out of my very sight. . . .

Yet Devlin continuously asserts the presence of the mortal, literal, woman in conjunction with the mythical force:

I know there is one thing, which is you,
It is the unique
Which also in part is she,
You, not seen by her,
You, not to be reduced by my eyes' famine of her.[69]

Mythic belief, then, has not destroyed his love of the unique and literal; but has destroyed his fear of them.

Devlin viewed Ireland as well as himself as part of the pattern of mortality. "The Tomb of Michael Collins" reconciles the loss of this heroic leader in the same way as the anticipated loss of a loved woman, by perceiving the divine in the mortal:

Walking to vespers in my Jesuit school,
The sky was come and gone: "O Captain, my Captain!"
Walt Whitman was the lesson that afternoon —
How sometimes death magnifies him who dies,
And some, though mortal, have achieved their race.[70]

Devlin, reflecting back to the difficult time of 1927, does not write about the civil war that ravaged Ireland or even specifically about the hero-martyr, Collins, who might have brought unity. Instead, he celebrates Collins as one of the select: "O Lord! how right that them you love die young!" Devlin's removal from the strictness of the Irish literary scene probably made possible this sincere patriotic poem, one which would have been so difficult for someone to write who still struggled with nationalism and internationalism.

Understandably, Devlin did not become one of the people he wrote of in "Lough Derg" for whom "All is simple and symbol in their world,/The incomprehended rendered fabulous." He was a civilized European who came to see the history of Ireland and the soul of man without the guilt inspired by fear and reticence so prevalent in his early poems.

*Poetry Ireland* and *Irish Writing* also served
to increase the health of the Irish literary world
by giving considerable attention to the poets of
Northern Ireland. So often during their publication these periodicals elicited a beauty and calmness that is
almost unseen in Ireland today with its riots and battles in the
North and the literary eagerness in the South. Roy McFadden
from the North illustrates the internationalism during the early
numbers of *Irish Writing* in a poem about W. B. Yeats called "In
Drumcliffe Churchyard":

> Not in Drumcliffe, Yeats, are you today.
> They've brought your skeleton to Irish clay
> For Irish worms to pick at; but you write
> Your signature elsewhere, beyond the trite
> Observances of country and creed,
> In time and place where there is genuine need.[71]

Unlike Devlin, McFadden entered willingly into the literary wars.
And in so doing, he developed the conversational tone which
typifies the present manner. In this poem it is modified only by
the clear and obvious rhymes that were probably done under the
influence of Yeats's own ironic verse.

John Hewitt, another poet of the North, appeared often in
the periodicals. Later Northern poets, John Montague and Seamus Heaney, published in the revived *Poetry Ireland*. Like their
elders, they recognize the importance of Dublin and the South to
any Irish poet. All find that being of the North will involve them
increasingly in the culture of that most troubled part of Ireland.
But the internationalists' concern with Western culture encourages them to view their existences in non-Irish contexts. John
Hewitt's "Awareness of Time" begins with mention of Eliot,
Morris, and figures from earlier French and English literature. Yet
the Northerner's uneasiness when away from the condition of his
land intrudes to bring the subject directly to Ireland and the
inability of those who are not Irish to understand "the wandering
Irish who carry their slums":

> But the answer they do not give, are unable to give
> not having the doom of the data in their bones,

> Being orderly logical men,
> not born in an attic close to the wandering moon,
> is that we here are haunted, hagridden, bewitched. . . .[72]

Understandably, a poet of worth and social significance would find his way, if Irish, into *Poetry Ireland*. David Marcus, and the other editors, made them not simply welcome but necessary.

Neither *Poetry Ireland* nor *Irish Writing* provided the Northern poet with the organ he needed — one a great deal more insular than these could allow themselves to be. For a while, before blood was let in violent frequency in Bogside and Londonderry, the Northern poet may have thought the battle of Ulster anger could be fought outside the North, or he may have been tempted to base his poetic on other than political and sectarian terms. John Montague seems to have done both of these in his continuous concern with the second series of *Poetry Ireland* both as contributor and editor of one issue. His poems published there do not touch upon the problems of life in Ulster. Instead they concern the problems of life anywhere. "The Split Lyre," appearing in the volume he edited, combines the psychological and mythic reality so important to the poet of today, who is often drawn into the possible beauty of existence:

> An unaccountable
> desire to kneel,
> to pray, pulls
> my hands but
> his head is not
> a crown of thorns:
> a great antlered
> stag, pity
> shrinks from
> those horns.[73]

Here, the recognition of the similarity between Orpheus and Christ turns into the difference between the two. Such a concern might well be, as it once was with Yeats, the basis of a beautiful poetic. But a troubled Northern Ireland will draw her poets home.

*Poetry Ireland* and *Irish Writing* not only presented the clear and well-established modes of thought and expression in the contemporary context. They also recognized and encouraged with sensible criticism the new, young writers. Pearse Hutchinson, later to become active in *Arena*, published his poem "The Peacock Speaks" in *Irish Writing*. Here he has a peacock in Phoenix Park describe himself and then inquire:

> Children can see, can love, can marvel at, can praise
>   with shrill crow and handclap the splendor of
>   my tail outspread, flouting the ground, for they
> do not need yet a complex thought, a grey disguise
>   for gladness glowing through the eyes.[74]

His concern with the solitary being, differing from the mass of the population, develops into his major theme later with much bitterness. Here, though, nostalgia for the simpler time of childhood provides a gentler tone. Soon the pleasant, ameliorative images go and now seldom appear in Hutchinson's verse, except for translations. The death of the old *Poetry Ireland* did not, of course, contribute to this change; but both are symptomatic of what happened as the new poets abandoned any chance of the coterie.

That some of the main writers in *Arena* also published in the second series of *Poetry Ireland* illustrates a continuation of the policy David Marcus had made his critical dictum: publish the best regardless of what the poet's allegiances may be. Of course, since John Jordan edited the new series, one would expect to find some poets from *Arena* included. Though he would be receptive to the poets of *Arena* because he and they have been and continue to be on friendly terms at McDaid's, one must recognize that John Jordan is a critic and editor of merit. Leland Bardwell and Michael Hartnett published good poems here. And Jordan included poems by Macdara Woods and Paul Durcan, who share with others an interest in the coterie that exists at McDaid's, partially as a memory of Kavanagh.

Much seems to have been expected by writers and editors; and these two periodicals gathered the best of those writings.

Thomas Kinsella also published in the first series of *Poetry Ireland* and was reviewed there with sensitivity and complexity.

Tracing the moods and expressions of the modern Irish writer through the run of *Poetry Ireland* and *Irish Writing* has led in every way to Liam Miller's Dolmen Press, which revived *Poetry Ireland* for eight irregularly published issues. According to Miller, the periodical ended when the need for it did because other publications provided places for poets to publish.[75] That he replaced the periodical in his own publishing list with a series of small books, each devoted to a single poet, under the general title *Poetry Ireland Editions*, suggests another answer. The desire to be part of a literary group has not been strong for the writers considered in this study, and what attraction the coterie may have had for them waned. Though all are outsiders, all read and know the others, often with sympathy but seldom with charity or fondness. The obliteration of the aura of Yeats and Co. is almost complete, so one more rallying point begins to disappear. Since the example of the past becomes less important as the newer poets find their audiences and receive critical approval, no longer are they bound by the all too tenuous tie of mutual antagonism for the past. The growth into the future has rested largely with the Dolmen Press, which has continued the spirit and in many cases the writers of *Poetry Ireland* and *Irish Writing*.

### CHAPTER V

# The Dolmen Press

Liam Miller's Dolmen Press is the most important publishing house of contemporary literature in Ireland. Miller, unlike most of the other editors discussed, has not limited publication to works of a particular theme, tone, or genre. From the Dolmen have come several scholarly books and an important scholarly journal, *The Irish Book*. Popular books, such as a guide to Yeats country, have been published. Also appear new editions of important writings, such as *The Poems of Emily Lawless*. Some fiction has been published. By far the most significant publications at the Dolmen have been poetry. Though the bias of the press is definitely internationalist, no attempt is made to make the Irish adopt at least the patois of contemporary uniculture. Instead, publications from the Dolmen remind the Irish that their culture and writers are greatly varied and that Irishmen have travelled far, learned much, and remained conscious of themselves as members of a distinct culture.

*Austin Clarke*  Though the Dolmen has published works by such established names as Synge and Gogarty and by such recently noticed ones as Boland and Liddy, the publication of the writings of Austin Clarke best illustrates the contribution of this press to contemporary Irish culture. Austin Clarke is not a neglected poet, but his achievement in poetry had long been undervalued. Yeats passed him by and gave the sceptre to F. R. Higgins. Also, Clarke had in his book *Poetry in Modern Ireland* made himself a *persona non grata* by his only slightly qualified censure of the "modernists" such as MacNeice and Rodgers, of Devlin's intellectualized verse. His affinities were with the poetry of Colum, Synge, and Stephens.

He was early influenced by Ferguson and Herbert Trench: "Life itself was an epic struggle, for I had spent my childhood resisting the mightiest of fallen angels, intent on seizing my soul."[1] I doubt that any of the younger poets could, or would, make such a statement. Unlike theirs, Clarke's struggle for identity was to achieve, not lose, an Irish consciousness. He sees himself as part of the movement towards self-conscious Celtism, urged into being by the writings of Renan and Arnold. And Clarke's description of the Celtic Twilight describes his own verse: it provided an escape for poets "from the mighty law and order of English poetry into that shadowy world of subdued speech and nuance."[2]

His poem "O Love, There Is No Beauty" shows his adeptness in writing such poetry himself:

> Drag down your lonely hair
> On breasts no child has ever known, for it
> Will bring you happy sleep and peace. There is
> No peace within my words.[3]

The use of assonance and consonance in this poem is typical of Clarke's writing and shows his conscious linking of himself with the writers of the Twilight just as much as does his use of their favorite themes of loss and despair.

By writing about the old heroes, Clarke also strengthened his ties to the past, as in these words Fionn speaks to Diarmuid:

> Only her black hair
> Burns arrogant across the black ravine
> Of ruinous years," he stopped. Through a grey mist
> Of dream he saw girlish Grainne lean
> Utterly from the past and then he felt
> Her fingers quietly as dewfall prest. . . .[4]

Clarke's romantic longing for what may be called "traditional sanctity and loveliness"has made Grainne into that beauty itself which draws a man into remembering a temporary, therefore fragile, beauty.[5]

With his love of Ireland's past and his separation from it, he is a good example of what he saw as characteristic of poetry in the time of Yeats:

> But this dilemma is wider than poetry and has always been shown in the conflicting tendencies of the country itself; the divergence has been intensified since we are now enduring the painful and pleasant desire to conserve our tradition and develop the Irish language again, and in the equally powerful desire to industrialize ourselves, dam our rivers for energy, burn our bogs as fast as we can, and merge ourselves with the twentieth century.[6]

However, Clarke was not a contemporary of Yeats, but a younger poet during the time Yeats reigned. So to understand the above dilemma as it pertains to Clarke, one should substitute Yeats and Company for the "desire to conserve our traditions." Clarke made such a substitution in one of his poems:

> Grey stone for hedges
> Has bound the green plain
> Around branchy Coole and the manor,
> Where I came on Yeats
> Still picking salmon
> He grassed from the Lake of Jewels;
> I dipped in his plate
> Without praise, without wine,
> Though he asked me to come to his Castle.[7]

Clarke's acceptance of the Yeatsian view was just as qualified as Yeats's acceptance of Clarke, though Yeats might well have been very taken with some of the more recent poems. However, earlier ones, such as "The Cattle-drive in Connaught," employed old themes to give an edge to satiric observation. Though using the old story about Maeve and Aleel, Clarke wrote the poem because "great miserable droves from the cattle market of Dublin passed our garden gate every Thursday on their way to slaughter in England and affected me in dreams."[8]

*Pilgrimage* is structured in the same way. As the notes show, the poems are a careful and learned re-creation of and invention from old stories and figures: St. Brigid, Queen Gormlai. But of especial interest is Clarke's recasting of the story of the woman of Beare, an old woman who contrasts the pleasures of youth with the "privation and suffering of her old age."[9] Her story suggests to him a contemporary parallel, which also indicates a difference between him and his elders:

> The drama of racial conscience did not attract our elder poets of the Celtic Twilight, though it particularizes that Gaelic poetry with which they were not acquainted at first-hand. That drama has become intensified now, the immodesty of present-day female dress is denounced in virile pastorals, and our Parliament passes laws against temptations, the pleasures of dancing and courting. Novels which are liable "to incite passion" are banned and the present writer is among the Irish novelists placed on the condemned list.[10]

Unlike the generation before him, Clarke does not contrast the present with an idealized past.

Clarke was, and so remains, a political liberal who anticipates a time in the future that will be less corrupt and unjust than the present. Yeats anticipated the *return* of such an age. Their poems about the Troubles illustrate their differences. In "Meditations in Time of Civil War" Yeats surrounded himself with things he understood, steady and predictable things, as designated by the titles of each section of the poem: "Ancestral Houses," "My House," "My Table," "My Descendants," "The Road at My Door," "The Stare's Nest by My Window." All led him to the creation of "a changeless work of art."[11] Clarke's poem about the Black and Tans and the Civil War is quite different:

> The thousand tales of Ireland sink: I leave
> Unfinished what I had begun nor count
> As gain the youthful frenzy of those years;
> For I remember my own passing breath,
> Man's violence and all the despair of brain
> That wind and river took in Glenasmole.[12]

Clarke remains an important link between the present and the source of modern Irish literature, as John Montague has observed: " . . . the fact that he is the last representative of the intellectual idealism of the national movement makes his comment all the more savagely appropriate: a twentieth century Austin after the Fianna, remembering the days before the cleric's bell put the fear of God into our public representatives."[13]

Clarke's poetry results from bases which were established before most of the young poets were born. Too frequently, though, the relevance of his poetry to the present has been overlooked; and he has been constricted to the past:

> Clarke is an old-style "anti-clerical," an old-style Republican, an old-style fighter for minorities, an old-style balloon-pricker, an old-style relisher of bawdry."[14]

John Jordan, in making this observation, intended to explain why Clarke had been, unjustly, overlooked by writers in the new mode. The appraisal is accurate, and until recently Clarke seems to have been intent on avoiding any statement which might qualify it. His censorious review of Ezra Pound's letters for *The Bell* in 1952 blames Pound for encouraging the "'tough' school."[15] Rather than view Clarke as a man limited to the past, it is more accurate to view him as one, at the time, limited to the processes of thought of the past.

His recent poetry dealt openly and radically with politics and morality. Even his poetic became freer. As Richard J. Loftus observed:

> Gone are the backdrop of medieval Ireland, the neopagan ideals, the occasional burst of comic humor. What remains is a savage rage that Ireland has not known since Swift in the seventeenth century and the Gaelic bards of an earlier age.[16]

Even Loftus, though, has not assessed the radical course of Clarke, one which is slightly suggested in "The Paper Curtain," a poem about contemporary Yugoslavia:

> This was at last the happy land
> Which Blake and William Morris saw in visions,
> Here angels of dissent might make a safe landing,
> For Roman Catholic, Moslem, Orthodox
> Soon had to end their theological divisions,
> No longer squabble over doxologies
> And dogma.[17]

In this enlightened Communist country, Clarke thought he had found "that Utopia" where bikini-wearing young people delighted in the world and their bodies. Here he thought he had found a freedom from repression and a tolerance that would have brought joy to Queen Gormlai and countless others who had existed within a religion and an ethic so narrow as to pervert all that is beautiful.[18]

Communism, a belief and a politics without traditional sanction, fulfilled the Romantic's dreams: a country finding a joy that is usually reserved for a man and a woman very much in love. Though predicted by Utopian visionaries, the form of government in Yugoslavia had not previously existed, indicating Clarke's willingness to free himself from past experience. With a feeling much like sorrow, I read his note to this poem: "When I set down these impressions after the P.E.N. Congress at Bled, I was not aware that a Jugo-slav writer had been held for years in captivity."[19] Although young writers, especially those who reached maturity after World War II, grew up in a world that would not allow such optimism as Clarke's, nor perhaps such disappointment, they have a tie with him. But from the most important theme in the writing of Austin Clarke begins, probably unconsciously, the central theme of contemporary Irish poetry: however temporary and wherever found, love is the most perfect experience men and women can have.

Clarke had always implied this significance of love. In *Old-Fashioned Pilgrimage* he presents explicitly an order of life based on the necessity of love, or at least charity. In a poem about Ezra Pound, he reflects how he had earlier "pooh-poohed" Pound's poems and his brash approach to Yeats and Eliot, as well as his enthusiastic discoveries of Europe. Then he remembers Pound's continued protest, "While Spender wrestles with his fire-hose; In vain, Auden becomes a choir-boy":

Rhyme, echo the name of Ezra Pound
Whom the war capitalists impounded,
For miserable years he pounded
The wall of modern verse, expounded
The madness of dollar, franc and pound,
Forget the theories he propounded,
But praise the language he compounded.
The centuries are in that pound.[20]

Much like Auden summing up the career of Yeats, Clarke attempted to praise Pound's craft while making his politics irrelevant.

Clarke protests not so much about the course of the contemporary world as the continuation of old hatreds, especially ones connected with religion. Seemingly the ecumenical movement has not changed Ireland's educated and important Roman Catholics. Counting Clarke, only two were present at the Protestant funeral services for Douglas Hyde, first president of Ireland.[21] This animosity is demonstrated at the opposite end of the intellectual spectrum by Roman Catholic children who shout at Protestant children, "Feckin' bastards, swaddlers, feckin' bastards!"[22] For Clarke, the Church retards Ireland's entry into the modern world not only by perpetuating the old Protestant-Catholic conflict, but also by rejecting scientific discoveries (such as birth control pills) which can improve the human condition. In "The Redemptorist" he presents a woman talking with her priest. She has had six children, but has been advised by her doctor that another pregnancy would be dangerous, perhaps fatal. Because she has not been pregnant in 10 months, the priest refuses to receive her confession and sends her home with the advice to "obey" her husband.[23] In a lighter poem, he writes of men and women using the contents of innocent looking packages from England:

With careful fingers, they unroll
The teated, pearly, glistening letter.
And women, too, are rightly armed
To meet them on that battlefield
Where in the dark tent they can feel
The foeman creep on knee and elbow.[24]

This poem, "Our Love Was Incorruptible," has the exuberance characteristic of many of Clarke's latest poems. The levity in the midst of seriousness occurs with greater frequency than before, and the pun is used with gusto.

Clarke's use of the pun but suggests the recent freedom of his poetics. He long used assonance and rhyme, but regularity of sound patterns controlled him. He has commented that discover-

ing the pun was like discovering rhyme all over again. He relates
his use of the pun to *rime riche* and is quite pleased with the
growing freedom and complexity of sounds in his poetry. He has
laughingly observed that the pun is now acceptable because Joyce
relied so heavily on it.[25] Clarke's poetry has, like that of the
younger poets, become conversational rather than simply narrative or celebratory as it had been.

In *Echo at Coole and Other Poems* the pun again overlays
serious themes with gusto. "In the Rocky Glen" recounts the
meeting between two young poets and Miss Mollie Garrigan:

> We felt the prick, a limpid
> Gaze mocking our double limp
> How could I have guessed
> I would soon be the guest
> Of the god, that his missile would glow
> Once more in the County of Wicklow
>> As I lay in bed,
>> Bow-twangled, ready,
> That soon with Molly beside
> Me, ache would be mollified?[26]

Much in keeping with the approach of the contemporary writer
Clarke insists on reminding Irishmen that all men, and women,
share in humanity.

No man is forever a national representative, and no man can
be expunged of desire or denied its gratification by any moral
decree. In "Phallomeda" he even insinuates that the ancient beliefs of Ireland give precedent for modern man to seek his love:

> Anticipating Rabelais,
> They wrote of the god who lay
> With loveliness. I copy that lay,
>> Applaud their disobedience.[27]

The pun, of course, is on lay, the vernacular for intercourse and
the literary for a short story in verse. Clarke in his poem simulates
both; and by his method fits himself to Irish tradition, as he
explains in a note:

I have changed this ancient tale slightly by introducing a well-known Greek goddess into it, instead of an Irish one. In several stories of the Fianna, a champion arrives from Greece to challenge all.[28]

This easy and open association of his writing with that of the past is the most important difference between Clarke and the younger poets. In "Paupers" and "The House-Breakers" Clarke shows that his allegiance to the present is quite selective. He rejects the new which replaces grace and love with neglect. No longer are the tale-telling paupers of Gort rewarded as they had been:

> A lady came from seven woods, a lake,
> Bringing the inmates twist, snuff, apples,
> She took their minds away in a basket,
> Left them on feast-days a curranty cake.[29]

Even though he described himself as "trespassing" when he was among the company Yeats and Lady Gregory gathered, he did not shun or senselessly attack them for their neglect. And he wrote forcefully of the destruction, called progress, of the signs of the past:

> Mayor, Alderman and councilors detect
> Georgian crack and strain in Merrion Square;
> Before they can be found. Young architects
> Copy our modern plans with ruler, square.
> Contractors nod. Has anyone been squared?
> Official, night-student from our Technical
> School? Iron balustrade, high fanlight, storey,
> Are gone. New glass and concrete end their story.[30]

Clarke's respect for honesty and beauty, for traditions that ennoble man, for people who have fought to free the mind of hatred would lead him to defend even people such as Yeats, who passed him over.

Clarke did much to liberate modern Irish poetry, though he himself could not enter with ease into the way of life and art he furthered. The reasons are two: first, he is bound to the past because he lived when the Irish Literary Renaissance and the nationalist movement were at their most powerful. His reaction to "Sir John Mahaffy, Provost of Trinity," illustrates his uneasiness with the Anglo-Irish establishment of the past.[31] Second, Clarke does not trust the present to preserve what is good from the past and suggests that the passionate love which has been the subject of much of his poetry has lost value for the present.

Clarke, seen in terms of his view of the present, is much more complex than even such a sympathetic observer as John Jordan has noticed: "Clarke is an old-style 'anti-clerical,' an old-style Republican, an old-style fighter for minorities, an old-style balloon-pricker, an old-style relisher of bawdry."[32] What Jordan has not mentioned is the basis from which each of these attitudes arises: Clarke's love of humanity. When this love receives impediment because of social, political, or religious problems, he reacts with poems which reflect quite well Jordan's view. "In O'Connell Street" is such a poem:

> I saw a procession of forty
> Or more poor people, shabby, ill-fed,
> Struggling along with hope, unfed-up,
> In the middle of the street, some holding
> Torn bits of paper and old cardboard;
> Few on the pavement, hardly a car.
> 'Our babies die!' 'We have no homes.'
> I read their grief.[33]

Always Clarke attacks because of the offense to humanity such people make. His concern with man differs from that of his younger colleagues mainly in being directed at the Irishman rather than at man as a member of the human race, part of which happens to be in Ireland. Another significant difference between Clarke and the younger writers occurs in the nature of their satiric attacks. Often the younger writers will involve themselves as part of what must be censured. Clarke separates himself. When talking with Clarke, I mentioned that his poetry seemed to me of two types: the celebration of love and attacks of savage indignation on any power that would destroy or corrupt love. He replied, "Yes, that's always been my way."[34]

*Thomas*
*Kinsella*

Thomas Kinsella is a contemporary Irish-man, though Dubliner is a more exact term, who came into maturity without the romantic dreams of the revolutionaries. He grew up with the failure of the 1916 Rebellion as an established fact, with certain knowledge of man's inability to live by any single principle, heroic or not. Kinsella's course is representative of Irishmen today: acceptable family, school, and career (civil servant). Only his genius separates him from innumerable contemporaries, making him so often the articulator of what many feel and might understand if they had Kinsella's complexity and dedication. Like them, Kinsella desires to be part of a living culture and a responsible nation; like them, he desires the happiness and ease of a quiet and complete homelife. Simple enough demands. But man must struggle against all unforeseen pain and defeat to achieve any of them.

In *Another September*, his first major collection, the poems are deft, relevant, and familiar. "Soft, To Your Places" sets an early Yeatsian tone, indicating that even as independent a poet as Kinsella had to struggle to be himself:

> Soft, to your places, animals,
> Your legendary duty calls.
>     It is, to be
> Lucky for my love and me.
>     *And yet we have seen that all's*
> *A fiction that is heard of love's difficulty.*[35]

Nothing here surprises; form and theme are familiar: easy rhymes tell the world love is a wonderful thing. The skill is undeniable, as is equally true of the balladesque "In the Ringwood":

> I kissed three times her shivering lips.
> I drank their naked chill.
> I watched the river shining
> Where the heron wiped his bill.
> I took my love in my icy arms
> In the Spring on Ringwood Hill.[36]

73

The uneasiness of this poem is abated by the familiar vocabulary, allowing the reader to withdraw from whatever may be the real experience of the poet. To the credit of Kinsella, however, he did not in all probability intend the poem to be a convenient reference for the reader. He intended to show that men have similar experiences regardless of the century.

Though often with astonishing effects, Kinsella's poems in *Another September* appear to be the results of brashness rather than confidence. No form seems unapproachable to him, and none seems his own. But Irish poetry would be the poorer if these poems, so evocative of their time, did not exist. The absence of "First Light," for instance, would retard the growth of a native and contemporary Irish poetry:

> Whereupon all manner of birds
> Exploded across the estuary, Winds
> Opened out white leaves:
> A stylus, guided by the horizon, printed and mirrored.
> For reply, I find I am left
> With an unanswerable dawn upon my hands.[37]

This captured Irish dawn is a memory worth retaining. *Experiences*, more than any other term, indicates the tie between Kinsella and his contemporaries. Like them, he has been concerned with presenting as directly as possible his experience. What needs to be seen, however, is that much more than the internationalists, Kinsella is concerned with a cultural experience.

In *Downstream* Kinsella controls diction without the obvious designs of the earlier poems and has more clear and literal themes, though a more complex statement can occur. The tone of the poems is, generally, the slightly acrid one of much good modern verse. "Prologue," which begins *Downstream*, provides a basis in the self for the anxiety which touched earlier poems, such as "Baggot Street Deserta":

> I wonder whether one expects
> Flowing tie or expert sex
> Or even absent-mindedness
> Of poets any longer. Less

Candor than the average,
Less confidence, a ready rage,
Alertness when it comes to beer. . . .[38]

Kinsella understands the difficulty of a vocation in which the role
one plays is predicted and by most people considered irrelevant.
Poets belong in anthologies, on shelves, in cemeteries. They
certainly don't need to be running about, mucking up the world
with their impatience and anxiety.

Kinsella's poems are about people and events relevant to his
own life. In "A Country Walk," Kinsella begins with an attitude
and action common to men:

Sick of the piercing company of women
I swung the gate shut with a furious sigh,
Rammed trembling hands in pockets and drew in
A breath of river air. A rook's wet wing
Cuffed abruptly upward through the drizzle.[39]

The walk takes him past signs of Ireland's struggles with the
Normans, the English in 1916; and he is carried on by the flow.
Seemingly, the poem continues in skillful and interesting verse
the approach of the internationalists: rejection of a society that
could only react to alien violence. Kinsella gave the poem unexpected value by suggesting the Stations of the Cross in the structure of the poem.[40] He consciously builds mythic, in this case the
Christian, overtones into his poetry without losing the personal,
confessional theme that is to characterize his poetry. "Mirror in
February" describes the poet shaving and thinking of his past
youth and his present life now that he has reached "the age of
Christ."[41] The parallel with Christ is to indicate basic and unalter-
able patterns in the life of man.

The personal life of Kinsella is important in his poetry, the
illness of his wife, his struggle to write with honesty and determi-
nation, his desire to be an important poet. But he does not
separate his life from the course of his culture, even though his art
has taken him from Ireland to America. "Downstream" illustrates
large social concern:

75

> The phantoms of the overhanging sky
> > Occupied their stations and descended;
> > But for an instant, to the starlit eye,
> The slow, downstreaming dead, it seemed, were blended
> > One with these silver hordes and briefly shared
> > Their order, glittering.[42]

All life, but especially Kinsella's, becomes the subject of the poem, as time carries man on without revealing a purpose. Unlike so many of the internationalists writing immediately after World War II, Kinsella never considers disquiet simply as an occasion for ironic attacks. It becomes a force in which he must find the pattern or be forever directionless in a society that cannot itself commit self-analysis.

Poems in *Wormwood* often closely resemble typical Irish Catholic thought, which in its Jansenist way separates spirit and body. This volume has its source in the poet's personal pain, which seems so pervasive that Kinsella cannot consider it simply as a momentary and accidental condition. He must reconcile the absence of joy in his life by finding a purpose for what has happened to him. The Irish recourse to Jansenism to explain a bewildering problem does not negate the possibility of wide relevance for these poems. The prefatory note expresses the sentiment of everyone who has sought joy and instead found pain:

> But if we drink the bitterness and can transmute it and continue, we resume
> in candor and doubt the only individual joy — the restored necessity to
> learn. Sensing a wider scope, a more penetrating harmony, we begin again in
> a higher innocence to grow toward the next ordeal.[43]

Such hope seems slight, but no more can occur without the existence of a pervasive ontological system. Kinsella needs to believe that he is part of a pattern of existence that has purpose and value. The dilemma is to remain human and yet have purpose.

Many of the poems in *Wormwood* are domestic, rather than expressly cultural. Even so, a changed view of existence within the culture is implicit. Another poem called "First Light" appears but resembles the one from *Another September* in name only:

Upstairs a whimper or sigh
Comes from an open bedroom door
— A child enduring a dream
That grows, at the first touch of day,
Unendurable —
And lengthens to an ugly wail.[44]

Earlier, Kinsella had scant reason to question the direction of his
life; but through pain and awareness, came uneasiness and the
belief that his life might not be propelled by unseen yet real forces
of culture. The image of a child crying at dawn turns to pain and
ugliness in Kinsella's hand. In "Wormwood" a dream reveals the
same pain:

The two trunks in their infinitesimal dance of growth
Have turned completely about one another, their join
A slowly twisted scar . . . that I recognize . . .
A quick arc flashes sidewise in the air,
A heavy blade in flight. A wooden stroke:
Iron sinks in the gasping core.
            I will dream it again.[45]

The sense of pain could be left as simply personal in these
poems. No matter what the subject, at a given point in his writing
Kinsella's approach will be similar. In an essay "The Irish Writer,"
written in 1966, he described his tie to the past:

This is done as well by a broken tradition as by a whole one, however painful,
humanly speaking, it may be. I am certain that a great part of the significance
of my own past, as I try to write my poetry, is that the past is mutilated.[46]

The same awareness is communicated in the poems; and in all he
struggles to heal the wound, to bring unity of self and culture.
With little, but real, hope Kinsella turns his attention to what can
be done to bring joy and unity to his people.

Kinsella, conscious of his relationship to Irish complexity,
opted for a tie to the past based on the mere Irish rather than the
Anglo-Irish: ". . . Yeats stands for the Irish tradition as broken;
Joyce stands for it as healed — or healing — from its mutila-
tion."[47] The problem of the untold, perhaps unknown, offense
that brings severe and extensive punishment is common to both

Joyce and Kinsella. For Kinsella, as for Joyce, the psychological and physical experience of man is a large part of his conception of self:

> A man in his life shares more with all men than he does with any class of men, in eating, sleeping, loving, fighting and dying; he may lack the sense of tradition and still share most of the human experience.[48]

Accepting this view, Kinsella prepares for a development long implicit in his poetry: search for patterns, perhaps allegorical, that underlie all human existence.

The poems in *Nightwalker* indicate the path of transmuted bitterness. In "Ballydavid Pier" Kinsella reflects on the shells of crabs, bones of fish, and foetus of a sheep in the ocean:

> Allegory forms of itself:
> The line of life creeps upward
> Replacing one world with another,
> The welter of its advance
> Sinks down into clarity,
> Slowly the more foul
> Monsters of loss digest. . . . [49]

The misbirth will be consumed by forms of life more able to exist, and Kinsella is left to ask, "Does that structure satisfy?" He answers obliquely in the last stanza when the Angelus is rung, and the notes carry across the bay, which will empty in time, and disturb nothing. The process is inexorable but not malignant. Death becomes an introspection, an insularity.

Similarly, Kinsella presents Dublin as broken from life and unwilling to associate itself with the healing force, the life force:

> A theatre for the quick articulate,
> The organized genteel, their artful watchers . . .
> Malice as entertainment, Asinine feast
> of sowthistles and brambles! And there dead men
> Half hindered by dead men, tear down beauty.[50]

Much of the poetry in *Nightwalker* concerns the debilitating life of Ireland, Dublin in particular. Dublin becomes the new city of the dead as Kinsella presents his ancestors' leaving the country for Dublin and his own leaving Dublin:

Dublin under the Georges . . .
>                    Stripped of Parliament,
>    Lying powerless in sweet-breathing death-ease
>                    after forced Union.
>    Under a theatre of swift-moving cloud
>    Domes pillared, in the afterglow —
>    A portico, beggars moving on the steps — [51]

In both cases, the continued life necessitated the move. The dead, the viciously introspective, must be left behind.

In "Nightwalker," Kinsella censures the Ireland that has developed through successive wars and compromises: a closed system consisting of a Church that provides servants for the government:

>                    Adolescents,
>    Celibates, we offer up our vows
>    To God and Ireland in Her name, grateful
>    That by our studies here they may not lack
>    Civil servants in a state of grace.[52]

The government of his country as surely as the cultural tradition is not linked to a living past. The "broken tradition" touches all; and Kinsella concludes, "I only know things seem and are not good."[53] Wherever he looks, at self or nation, no definite purpose directs:

>                    Is it not right to serve
>    Our banks and businesses and government
>    As together we develop our community
>    On clear principles with no fixed ideas?[54]

Profit is the means and end of the modern nation. No sense of service exists.

For a writer in a more impersonal culture writing may be separated from the past of the country. But not in Ireland. There every writer must be judged by the past, especially the recent past of Yeats and Joyce. Kinsella consciously broke loose from this part of the past, as did his contemporaries. However, only in *Nightwalker* does he manage to be free. He neither copies nor caustically rejects Yeats, but comes to see him as a poet against whom he need not be measured but one who deserves respect, not simply necrophiliac curiosity. "Death in Ilium" constructs a classical metaphor Yeats would have appreciated:

Attention and power relax,
Truth deserts the body:
Hector among his books
Drops dead in the dust.

The tireless shadow-eaters
Close in with tough nose
And pale fang to expose
Fibre, weak flesh, speech organs.

They eat but cannot eat.
Dog-faces in his bowels,
Bitches at his face,
He grows whole and remote.[55]

The consideration with which Kinsella treated Yeats, while at the same time relieving him of contemporary relevance, becomes understandable in "Magnanimity (*For Austin Clarke's seventieth birthday*)." In spite of the enmity between Clarke and Yeats, they appear much alike in Kinsella's poem. Both considered Coole to be not only a place of refuge for artists but a source of poetry. As Kinsella walked the grounds with Clarke and looked at the famous tree which is now surrounded with wire for protection, he reflected:

I am sure that there are no places for poets,
Only changing habitations for verse to outlast. . . .
Houses shall pass away, and all give place
To signposts and chicken-wire.
                              A tree stands.
Pale cress persists on a shaded stream.[56]

Though places have great significance in Kinsella's poetry, they are not in themselves sacred.

Like Joyce, Kinsella sees place as important because of its associations, such as the Martello Tower that has become a metaphor for the artists:

Watcher in the tower, be with me now
At your parapet, above the glare of the lamps.
Turn your milky spectacles on the sea
Unblinking; cock your ear.[57]

Unlike Joyce, however, Kinsella does not make place into a
metaphor of the human condition. Place can occasion particular
knowledge and experience because of the activity that seems
natural there, not because the place has an indigenous quality
which controls man. Man must conceptualize and try to bring
himself and his culture to health. Purposeless destruction is the
only other recourse.

The most complete affirmation of craft and life in *Nightwalker* is "Phoenix Park." True to his style, Kinsella struggles to
avoid the old cliches, but they peep in to lend an air of disunity:
"One stays or leaves. The one who returns is not/the one, etcet-
era. And we are leaving."[58] Contrived, to be sure. But Kinsella's
theme in the poem is that one must develop willed action through
understanding the forces of control. For a Dubliner, Phoenix
Park should bring to mind the Invincibles and Ireland's struggle to
be free. To Kinsella, the place recalls a walk with someone he
loves. Kinsella's commitment is different from that of the traditional association, making the park an historical allusion. He
struggles for new value and finds it through his expression of love
and desire for a woman.

The poem proceeds to draw together the personal life of the
poet and the life of the culture. Kinsella, so often, casts himself in
the role of a mythically inspired being whose own well-being
depends upon the health of his land, with the reverse being
implied. As he prepares to leave the park, Ireland by association,
he finds his willed action begins to bring into being an existence
more basic and pervasive than his and the woman's:

A few ancient faces
Detach and begin to circle. Deeper still,
Delicate distinct tissue begins to form.[59]

This flesh, unlike that of the misborn sheep in "Ballydavid Pier,"
is alive. The broken tradition is being healed. Man and woman are
finding value. The poet begins his trek to the next ordeal.

During Kinsella's pain and growth, his interest in translating ancient Irish literature has remained constant. This concern differentiates him sharply from confessional poets of other countries. Also, his approach to the past is distinctly part of his time, bearing slight resemblance to that of Irishmen earlier in the century. For him, the tradition is broken; and he is separated from the past: "The greatness of the loss is measured not only by the substance of Irish literature itself, but also by the intensity with which we know it was shared: it has an air of continuity and shared history which is precisely what is missing from Irish literature in English or Irish in the nineteenth-century and today."[60] He is trying to understand what the man and the community of the past were like and to find terms, if any exist, by which the break may be crossed.

Kinsella's first translations to be published were brief ones from the Christian culture of early Ireland. "Thirty Three Triads" records the code of life among the pre-Christian Irish, modified by a later recorder who was Christian. The mixture of ethics pleases in describing a community with spiritual worship and human life in concord:

> The three with the lightest hearts:
>   a student after reading his psalms, a young lad
>   who has left off his boy's clothes for good, a
>   maid who has been made a woman.

and

> Three coffers whose depths are shrouded in mystery:
>   that of a prince, that of the church, that of a well
>   patronized poet.

Then, too, are instructions for living well within the highly stratified and interdependent society of the pagan Irish:

> Three who throw their freedom away:
>   a lord who sells his land, a queen who takes up with a boor,
>   a poet's son who deserts the craft.[61]

In "Faeth Fiadha: The Breastplate of Saint Patrick," Kinsella translated a hymn designed to protect monks. For Kinsella, however, it protects the soul of man: "And here is the faith's trunk armour, to guard the body and soul from demons, desires, and demented men. Devils will not fly in the face of him who recites it every day with his entire mind on God. It will protect him against poisons and jealousies, cherish him from a terrible end and armour his soul after death."[62] Man belongs to a community bound together by a living faith. Kinsella would be attracted to this work since his own poetry is troubled by the disunity of men.

*The Tain*, Kinsella's most important translation, began when he translated the story of Deirdre. In Kinsella's version, Deirdre lives with Chonchobar after he killed Naisi, the man she loved. She killed herself only after Chonchobar grew tired of her and was going to give her to Eogan. Kinsella is not the first to tell the story with this ending, but his version of it is by far the most readable and has the best chance of replacing the more popular one.

In a note to the *Tain* he suggested his basic reasons for the new translation:

> The versions I could find were generally dull, and I emerged with conviction that Lady Gregory's 'Cuchulain of Muirtheme', though only a paraphrase, gave the best idea of the Ulster stories. This merely emphasized the dearth, for her book, even as a paraphrase, seemed unreliable in some important ways, refining away the coarse elements and rationalizing the monstrous or gigantesque; as well as this, the *Tain Bo Cuailnge* — the prose epic which is the centre-piece of the Ulster cycle — seemed inadequately represented.[63]

Kinsella wants to supply an accurate and readable text of Ireland's great epic. But underlying this purpose is a desire to correct the misunderstanding of the past created by the writers of the Literary Renaissance and add to the understanding of their past by the Irish themselves, rather than allow a continuation of the disunity because of the work of the Anglo-Irish.

Kinsella and his contemporaries are no closer to the warrior ethic of Cuchulain's time than were Yeats and his fellows. But writers now can accept a varied and foreign experience more easily. For instance, Cuchulain's killing of his own son does not appeal to Kinsella, though he must respect the code of that time and try to give an accurate narrative:

> They went down into the sea to drown each other, and the boy submerged him twice. Then Cúchulainn turned and played the boy foul in the water with the *gae bolga*, that Scathach had taught to no one but him. He sent it speeding over the water at him and brought his bowels down around his feet.[64]

Lady Gregory and Yeats replaced the warrior's ethic that would make Cuchulain offer to kill his son with a more modern, and less bloodthirsty, cause for the action. Cuchulain was forced to kill his son against his will by social pressure. The romantic conflict again: the beautiful soul corrupted by society. Kinsella could not continue such a version of the story; for that would be antagonistic to his own realist's assertion of flawed humanity, not society alone, as the source of man's patterns of behavior.

Kinsella does not avoid subjects simply because they are unattractive to him or the result of an aesthetic he does not share. For instance, few modern writers have made the epic catalogue part of their writing. But because it occurs often in the *Tain*, Kinsella translates without the presumptuous suggestion that the poet nodded. Just as he attempts to be honest in examining his own life, Kinsella presents the complex and foreign world of the pagan Irish. The humor of the *Tain* does not occur in the earlier versions because the writers then had an image of self to be vindicated by the ancient literature which did not include anything as chaotic as a varied tone. In Kinsella's version the humor occurs, often at times of death, as when Redg, the satirist, succeeds in getting Cuchulain's javelin:

> Then Redg said he would take away Cúchulainn's good name unless he got the javelin. So Cúchulainn flung the javelin at him and it shot through his head.
> "Now, that is a stunning gift!" the satirist cried.[65]

In Kinsella's *Tain* are men who laugh, weep, eat, sleep, make love, die as is fitting to the occasion.

The significance of Kinsella's translations is yet to be proved, but the reasons for them and the stylistic achievement they represent are clear. Kinsella has looked at his cultural past without trying to shape it by ethics and aesthetics foreign to it. He would not have done this, in all probability, unless it served his own needs. Kinsella, being inclined to write highly personal and introspective verse, needed the discipline of a tradition outside him-

84

self, a living tradition against which to measure himself, if not be directed by. Translating writing from the time when the writer's role and responsibility were determined by social dictums having their source before the memory of man gave Kinsella close acquaintance with the possibility of human life. Never suggested, though, is an ideal life, rather a different idea of right behavior. As is true for man today, the epic hero cannot abide without disunity in a code of behavior. Man will violate any sanctity because of his unfixity of purpose, the uncontrollable complexity of drives. Out of loss and destruction, victory and celebration, joy and pain, man must accept his life and sometimes structure it. That Thomas Kinsella can only try, with some small success, to structure life by a purpose other than himself simply means he lives in his own time. Now no single belief fills men, and one believes that out of the pain and joy will come a pattern which will lead man to understand why he must endure and transmute ordeal after ordeal.

*Desmond* *O'Grady* More than most of his contemporaries, Desmond O'Grady is the outsider. With friends, he went to Rome; and together they formed what may be called a colony of Irish expatriates. Concerned with contemporary poetry outside the confines of Irish antagonisms, they wrote with specific attention to the details of life during their own present. Understandably, such unabashed modernity would cause irritation in a land so aware of the past as is Ireland. John Hewitt's rejection of their techniques and themes is illustrative.[66] O'Grady's affiliation, if any, is with the avant-garde publications such as *Arena* and *The Holy Door*. He has been well and justly praised by John Jordan, who more than any other man knows the history of these Irish literary cliques.[67] Published by the Dolmen, he is included in the eclectic gathering of bards Liam Miller believes in. No other rationale for publication by the Dolmen exists, and Miller's taste is praiseworthy.

After an early withdrawal from Ireland into internationalism, perhaps O'Grady has also been able to see his country. He has not, however, been tempted to re-establish residence there. In *The Dark Edge of Europe* he is constantly concerned with the *nature* of his relationship to Ireland. "Was I supposed To Know?" leads the reader through a child's confusion, a young man's rebellion to a mature man's comprehension of his place in "some high guiding plan" which serves

> to lead me back to where,
> Again,
> With coffin smell of pew
> And criss of Cross
> Unwinking eyes of saints and hushed confession queue —[68]

Even this recognition of a tie with the culture of his homeland does not bring O'Grady snugly into the form and sound of his contemporaries' verse.

In "Afternoon" he describes what could be any town, but most assuredly is an Irish one:

> The voice on the radio — remote, unmelodic — gives news of events
> And things that are happening — urban expansion, rural improvements,
> Revolutions and riots, social reforms and new intellectual movements —
> In lands with more future than this one presents.

Suggesting an avant-garde concern, O'Grady does not limit himself to a fashionable pose. He touches a theme that has been a major one in every modern culture, but does so in terms that evoke the details of a people drawn fine by the enclosure of a rural community:

> Crack, and the shouts of men go up as a rat breaks cover
> To die by the stones and the longhandled sticks of exasperation,
> Back of the wagons in the stopped yards of the black, uneventful station —
> And just for a moment the waiting is over.[69]

O'Grady viewed the extensiveness of this lack of purpose quite sharply in "The Scattering." Often the censure carries the sound of Pound (whom O'Grady knew) and the exiles after World War II:

> not the right cause fought
> against the wrong people, not
>> *an old bitch gone in the teeth*
>> *a botched civilization*
> and not the sanctification of false martyrs.[70]

An accumulation of history from the words of men only serves to show how much time has passed and to indicate the impossibility of the old ways serving as guidance for present actions. Not even exile provides escape or hope as he metaphorically describes the sun setting

> on those left at home in Limerick on the Shannon River,
> down on Dublin at the corner of Golden Lane
> and Ship Street, down on rue Mouffetard and down forever
> on us all in Rome.[71]

The melancholy so often characteristic of the internationalists, especially of the exiles, pervades not only this but many of O'Grady's poems.

O'Grady, however, is neither simplistic in his approach nor insular when he writes about places or memories. In a poem recalling the history of Ireland and the life of Louis MacNeice as reflected in some of the dead poet's unpublished papers, O'Grady expresses an understanding of the way man is. Recalling Hugh O'Neil, who resembled MacNeice and O'Grady in being an exile, O'Grady ends the poem with a general comment on human life: which is prompted by the return of MacNeice s body to Ulster. All three men become involved in the process of life, exile, death.[72] The poem is specific, personal, but not simply evocative of a limited scene. O'Grady, unlike many, offers a large ontological structure which can guide or control the life of an individual, a culture, a country. He is not hesitant to assert the existence of such structures.

O'Grady, secure in the experience of life and unfearfully anticipatory of death, offers in this volume a mythopoeic answer to man today. Being aware that what today are labeled neuroses may once have been patterns of behavior, O'Grady tries to find within experience the behavioral basis. In "Land" he gives his characters traditional forms and sets them into a pattern of behavior that has divided men and women today into hostile camps, antagonized by sexual and emotional difference. Men and women cannot often merge into a quiet settled union. But to abandon life because love must risk pain and destruction is not O'Grady's answer:

> O husbandman, husbandman, lord of the nail and hammer,
> open your eyes to the grammar of lies a woman
> will wrap round your marriage finger in the most aphrodital
> manner
> to bed you, and then
> in the digging disguise of the copulate dark, be the fake
> butt of your fury and shake the wool on your thighs.
> O bury your love for your own sake in the chances love
> cannot take
> and button your eyes.[73]

The differences between toiler/lord and wife/goddess are real. Being inescapable, they become elementary to humanity.

In *The Dying Gaul*, O'Grady concerns himself even more explicitly with an approach to life invented by the pagan. The opening poem celebrates earth, love, and the seasonal cycle in multi-religious terms:

> This ancient earth, these laboured lands,
> announce love's annual mystery. The great
> mother bears her own salvation — though man's
> cross remains his seasons, his people, his death.[74]

The equations between individuals and figures of divine manifestation appear even more significantly than was true in *The Dark Edge of Europe*. O'Grady has made knowledge of destruction, loss, and pain integral to the course of his life and not an uneasiness to be shunned. He makes the destruction of his ancestors and his own destruction become the knowledge out of which he must sieve the value of life, and he finds within his own kind the force he must fear:

> All ruin bears witness, the stones cry out the price
> of all uprising. The noble perish, lost
> for the times' demands. The base still rule, increase
> their lot upon advantage, cull the cost
> and sell all gain back to the old deviser.
> Not by strangers but by our own we're crossed
> and murdered — in the name of the father, the son and the
> mother.[75]

The family itself, with the necessity that child replace father or avenge father, contains and communicates the ancient danger of destruction.

A poet who finds the religion of man in the process of life itself rather than in sanctuaries set aside from daily events would understandably find an oracle, or at least a wise man, outside the chapel. O'Grady knows Ezra Pound well, a man who must be the one described as delighting "in reading the world's mad signs." The prophecy tells of what is to come and explains the cause of the inevitable course:

> Though we all must one day meet our killer demon,
> chance all in combat, lose all and die,
> our loss still burns in trophies, yields our freedom. . . .[76]

Man will be destroyed. If he does not comprehend himself within his times and as part of all times, he will be destroyed by ignorance. He will be simply controlled by the flexing of history. If he comprehends, knowledge will separate him from his fellows and like Narcissus he will die in "alien streams." The latter, of course, is preferable for both the old man and his younger companion.

O'Grady does not leave his poetry removed from the life of his own time, having abandoned the contemporary for mythopoeic understanding. The many-headed hydra becomes the foreshadowing of the monster of today:

> Plundering like power, he's a pusher —
> angels, engines, you name it —
> eats men like air
> singly, in groups, whole nations.[77]

The state of mass identity threatens the hero's life. Such enjoyment as conformity offers is not, O'Grady observed, without praise and honor. Neither is it security against destruction. Instead, the destruction becomes a way of life, not a way of death. At the best, conformity to the modern structure offers quiet anonymity. At the worst, an incarceration similar to what the Jews found at Auschwitz, Buchenwald, Belsen; for in their ghettos, workers

> build towns, roads, general transport;
> crawl home at night
> a cockroach
> charred black as the Negro
> by the Man's furnace.[78]

This poem fits well the pattern of the internationalists in *Envoy* and *Arena*: guilt for repression and genocide, social concern, acceptance of any forceful and accurate word as suitable for poetry.

O'Grady's writing differs from most of what the internationalists wrote because it is based on a structured understanding of existence. Understandably he would be able to approach the poetry of Yeats without discomfort. Poem "30" in *The Dying Gaul* describes the statue which provided O'Grady with the title for this volume:

> The hour at last come round
>     the stroke that scores the kill
> taken, there follows a painless,
>     partly nostalgic withdrawl —
> a drag to the sideline — to a clean piece
>     of this world's dying ground.[79]

Recasting Yeats's "Its hour come round at last" in "The Second Coming," O'Grady exchanges, also, the birth of the "rough Beast" for the death of a Gaulish warrior.[80] But the purposes of the two poets are the same: to show the continuity of life.

O'Grady relates himself to a broken tradition. In it he finds the basis of communication among people who resist death in life. Looking in the "alien stream" of other cultures he made the most important discovery of the internationalists: because all lives follow or avoid the same pattern does not free anyone from the particularity of his own culture. And the last poem in the volume acknowledges O'Grady's lineage and his understanding of the festival of seasons in which all people can participate:

The dead unburdened, the year's
renewed. Man,
avenged, declares:
I am my father's son.[81]

O'Grady's own father and the sequential relationship of father and son have figured in this volume. However, O'Grady is not in this poem referring solely to his genealogical father. Pound and the Gaul, as well, are celebrated. The truth of what they have seen is acknowledged. The son celebrates the struggle of man, the life's failure of some, and death's conquest of others. Whatever the course, he recognizes that in all run the flaws of indecision and compromise. The flaws themselves are separations between man and life-giving ritual. The tradition which carries the ritual differs from country to country; but always when man corrects the flaw, he finds himself in the same mythopoeic land.

In his translating, O'Grady has poems more properly called versions than translations. He suggests the reason for his approach in the introduction to *Off License*:

Ezra Pound has said that the literature of a country should be translated afresh at least once every fifty years since the significance of language changes so rapidly.[82]

Pound, as some have accusingly said, did not follow assiduously the originals. In the works of both poets is an expression of what might have resulted if the translator were the original poet. Such an approach allows the poet/translator to retain his own identity in his own time.

In his translations from the Irish, O'Grady limits himself to two themes: Irish nationalism and courteous love. The patriotic poems present loyalty as making such a total claim on man that love of woman and life must be sacrificed. In the translation of "Naked I Saw You" by Patrick Pearse, both love and lust are repressed because the poet's life has a single, death-bound purpose.[83]

In "Donnagha White," an anonymous nineteenth-century poem, O'Grady again showed the sacrificial side of patriotism. The brother of a patriot executed by the British contrasts the way Donnagha White died with the simple pleasures he was meant for:

It was for no scaffold you were born —
But for cutting wheat and threshing corn,
For turning the plough both left and right
And turning the red clay into sight.[84]

Again the antithesis between life and patriotism occurs. In both poems, an order of existence based on union with the earth must be abandoned.

In "Kathleen, The Daughter of Houlahan" O'Grady translated a poem celebrating the personification of Ireland as a woman who calls men from field, hearth, and bed to oppose the British. Both the subject and the character are familiar in Irish literature, and in this version O'Grady stressed another dominant characteristic of Irish literature and culture. The pre-Christian and the Christian faiths of Ireland complement rather than conflict with one another. Kathleen will bear "the Royal Warrior Son" who will be another Finn. Finn is the ancient Irish hero who hibernates until a great crisis in Ireland awakens him. He is part of the culture of warrior clans, magical poets, and passionate women that Patrick seems to have had difficulty accepting. But in this poem, pagan and Christian unite.[85]

However, O'Grady does not posit a separate culture for Ireland, and in translating Irish poetry he does not retreat into a simplistic view of character distinctly Irish and nothing else. The majority of his translations from the Irish are poems which celebrate love within the tradition of Romance that once was widely spread throughout Europe. In his introduction, O'Grady suggested his concern with European experience: "The Armenian poems were made from prose translations done for me by a friend. My interest in them was the courtly love element they so strongly contain and which is so similar to the courtly love poetry of Ireland and other European countries."[86] The idea of such love controls the theme in "The Poet Loves from Afar," an anonymous poem from around the fifteenth century which praises a woman the poet cannot forget:

> If I had the choice and the pick of all women;
> The finest in Ireland, in Scotland and France;
> I'd like nothing more than a night's wild loving
> With that young one I saw at the crossroads dance.[87]

In the Armenian poems, as well, O'Grady indicates a love that is free and physical, not corrupted by concepts of sin. Often beauty, youth, and spring become subjects for praise of life. The frequent union of the three calls to mind the original poetry of O'Grady with the stressing of the seasonal cycle.

In his original poetry, O'Grady explicitly states an ontology which is but suggested in the translations. Beliefs which underlie those of revealed religion provide him with an identity that rejects the abstractions of self that developed from nineteenth-century religion and business. Romance and the fertility cycles provide him with direction. But O'Grady did not lose his own culture in any European mythologizing. Instead, he discovered through Ireland an entry into the broader culture.

*Richard*
*Murphy*

Richard Murphy's poems also express a separation between the poet and many of the people around him. Murphy is estranged by an intellectual commitment which gives many of his poems a Proustean removal. Not only the larger population's memory of the church and the Anglo-Irish government of his ancestors, but his memory of them as well marks him as different from the majority of the poets mentioned in this study.

Murphy's mention of the Anglo-Irish tradition and the ancestors who embodied it is without justification, amplification, or metaphoric extension. Until one sees that he regards life as a continuing but not repetitive process, some ambivalence occurs. In "Epitaph on a Fir-Tree" one is denied the readily grasped bias, so often characteristic of Irish writing. He writes of the cutting down of an imported fir tree planted ninety years before by bridesmaids at a wedding breakfast:

> Axes and saws now convert the evergreen
> Imperial shadows into deal boards,
> And let the sun enter our house again.[88]

The officers on the porch, the delicate girls, are recalled without nostalgia and without approbation. The people about whom he writes have beauty and have given joy. One does not see them as the absentee landlords who left the running of their estates to opportunists. This life, though past, he admires; and he loved the people who lived it. In an elegy for his aunt he again recalled a way of life that has passed:

> She bandaged the wounds that poverty caused
> In the house that famine labourers built,
> Gave her hands to cure impossible wrong
> In a useless way, and was loved for it.[89]

Murphy does not excuse the wealth of the owner and the plight of the poor, nor does he neglect the difference between the two. Whenever he comments, much is to be learned in a few words. The house with its duelling pistols, memorabilia of the Crimean, copies of Lever, Lover, Somerville and Ross belong to the past. His poem does not retreat into the lives of the dead but collects their memory as an estimable example of human endeavor in a past time.

Murphy's involvement in the memory of his family approaches what is called personal, even confessional, poetry. Because he does strive for detachment, however, noticeable ego-involvement is not often there. For example, in "Droit De Seigneur, 1820," he tells of a Protestant clergyman who went hunting for Ribbonmen, a rebellious group violently protesting the practices of the landlords. Sympathy is usually for the Ribbonmen, and so is Murphy's. However, he is more concerned with making his reader know and see what he writes about than with indoctrination. His description of a portrait of Cromwell in the rectory tells much: "One hand on the Bible, the other on a sword." The scene is further set by the rector's concern with cattle prices given in the *Connaught Journal*, with the seduction of a farm girl by a British soldier, and with the rector's explanation for his hunt: "Saving of property went with saving of souls."[90] After a single "young simpleton" had been captured and condemned to hang, all returned to order. But the abuse is clear in the poem, as is Murphy's theme that such injustice cannot interminably continue.

In technique, as well as in subject, Murphy's fondness is for a past when craftsmanship was prized. "The Last Galway Hooker" illustrates both. To make certain his efforts were not overlooked, he prefaced the poem with notes which explained the words used, the history of the boat, and the metrics of the poem. Of the latter: "The typical line has four stresses (though not of equal emphasis) which fall usually into two groups of two stresses each." The caesura is usually long.[91] After having evoked the joy and love of the men who had built and sailed this boat Murphy spoke of the man from whom he bought her:

And he never married, was this hooker's lover,
Always ill-at-ease in houses or on hills,
Waiting for weather, or mending broken trawls:
Bothered by women no more than by the moon,
Not concerned with money beyond the bare need,
In this boat's bows he sheathed his life's harpoon.[92]

This man, though in part controlled by increasing expenses, belonged to a past in which profit and scientific endeavor were foreign. The seaman, the ship, recall a past when grace, craft, and dedication were important, a time in contrast with the present.

Murphy's rejection of much of the change that has come in post-war times does not extend to the emerging nations of Africa. "The God Who Eats the Corn," written in memory of his father, presents with equal sympathy the graceful and cultivated life of his father, a man concerned with beauty, fruition of the good, and the improvement of man's existence ("My father, who was born in an Irish Rectory, retired from the British Colonial Service as Governor of the Bahamas and settled in Southern Rhodesia in 1950 on virgin land, where he established a farm and later a school for African children.") and the Africans, whose independence will terminate the usefulness of the white man.[93] The subject is a familiar one in Murphy's poetry, as is his theme: men, not systems, are valuable. He is a humanist in the modern sense with the older respect for the classics:

> While he prepares to fly to Ithaca
> The B.S.A. police hold rifle drill.
> A pyre kindles under *Pax Britannica*.
> He stays to build a club-room for the school.[94]

Like others among the contemporary Irish poets, Murphy gauges existence by the similarity of the individual to mankind in a large sense.

He does not codify humanity but searches for bases of agreement. But he does not share trauma-ridden guilt for the deaths of the Jews in World War II, for the hatred and deaths of innumerable blacks throughout the world, which characterizes much contemporary Irish poetry. Though he shares many of their attitudes, reacts to the contemporary world as do they, practices a psychological approach to poetry, concentrates on the image rather than the metaphor, his poetry is based on an inherited view of the world which the rest have either rejected or not shared in. Murphy has inherited a respect for service and an understanding of the bonds between man and his culture which many others lack or have come to hesitatingly.

In *The Battle of Aughrim*, Murphy's longest poem yet, all of his identifying characteristics become accentuated. And in the course of the poem, the history of Ireland has more importance than the history of the literature. During the time this poem was written, the war in Northern Ireland was building towards the fervor it now has, which undoubtedly affected Murphy's choice of subject and his treatment of it. Quite in keeping with his other writing, this poem examines the historical source of present existence.

Murphy's intended function of the poem, in terms of contemporary politics, is emphasized by the first section, "Now":

A Celtic cross by the road commemorates no battle
But someone killed in a car, Minister of Agriculture.
Dairy lorries on the fast truck-route rattle:
A girl cycles along the lane to meet her lover.[95]

The people oblivious to the significance of the area also receive a slighting treatment, seen in the curious parallel examples of the present. Murphy, as he has done before, writes of the present to discredit it. But in doing so he stresses the source of the condition in the past. Though the people may be unaware of why they react as they do, the effects can be perceived in Londonderry, where insults to the Queen recall "Bygone canon, bygone spleen."[96] Probably no war is fought without permanently scarring a country, but wars of racial origin do the most damage.

Murphy portrays the battle and Ireland's difficulties through an immediate and clear presentation of the scene, with no open personal involvement:

The army commander only speaks
French and Italian:
In ranks below colonel
His army only speaks Irish.[97]

But his poetry does not lack poignancy because of objectivity. The cruelty of the battle and its aftermath has a painful edge seldom found outside the sagas and the border ballads, as for instance when he tells of the death of a wolfhound that has stayed with the dead body of her Irish master:

A redcoat, stalking, cocks
His flintlock when he hears the wolfhound growl.
Her fur bristles with fear at the new smell,
Snow has betrayed her lair.
"I'll sell you for a packhorse
You antiquated bigoted papistical bitch!"
She springs: in self-defense he fires his gun.
People remember this.[98]

The irony of the British soldier's description of the dog is not humorous, even out of context. Today such bigotry has turned Belfast and Londonderry into battlegrounds.

*Richard*
*Weber*
Richard Weber illustrates well the Irish tradition as the contemporary writer has developed it. Like many of his elders and peers, he cannot approve the effect of the Church on the people. In "Summa Theologica" he echoes a familiar complaint:

> The time appointed,
> His thought upright,
> The husband claims
> His awful right.[99]

The bawdy puns, so reminiscent of Clarke's, do not soften the force of Weber's reprimand. Though the poem suggests Clarke's similar satire, Weber does not use the Freudian approach that often is Clarke's.

Instead, Weber clearly shows his place among the younger poets by avoiding the definiteness of a clearly defined methodology, in the sense of an identification of idea and approach, a specific source for answers. He attempts to present the condition without explanation or amplification. "Two Part Song" exemplifies this respect for distinctiveness of experiences and of expression:

> Neither of us is perfect: we nonetheless prefer
> Because we defectively love each other,
> To live separately, mutually aware.[100]

Richard Weber's second book of verse, *Stephen's Green Revisited*, is actually not always chronologically later than *Lady and Gentleman*. The first half of the volume contains poems written when he was quite young but not published until later. In these poems, the irritation with the repression of the Church again appears, as in "The Priest in the Train":

His coal black, polished shoes suggest a little
The archetypal, world deflecting devil's hoof,
But only, perhaps, by the contrary contraries
of a lax layman's faithless turn of thought.[101]

This quietly vicious poem seems gratuitous in its attack, that
being the assumption of knowledge of the nature of this particular
priest. But then for a fallen-away Christian like Weber (he says he
gave up the Church at 18 and took up pipe smoking) a priest is a
complex and definite stimulus of oppression and opportunism.[102]

Other memories of London appear in the early part of the
book as evidence of Weber's Irishness, not his desire for exile. In
"O'Reilly's Reply" the *persona* of the poem is a transient in London:

Let's say I love here, in a way,
Where the poet perfecting his poems before dark
May pick his writing paper from the litter in the park.[103]

Weber's travels have taken him to teach in two American
universities, but these too seem impermanent. He has returned
frequently to Ireland and has now bought a small lakeside cottage
in County Wicklow. There he goes when possible — for increasingly longer stays.

In an interview he gave while teaching at Mount Holyoke
College in America, he indicated his concern with writers in
several countries; but his emphasis was on two writers basic to his
own culture: William Butler Yeats and Austin Clarke. His concern with Austin Clarke is immediately obvious in his sardonic
attacks on Irish institutions, especially the Church and in the
punning rhymes he uses in these poems. His poem, "A Visit to
Bridge House," tells of one of his many visits with Clarke and
does so in lines with the loose assonance that typifies much of
Clarke's later verse:

I think of your art of giving life to language:
From graft with older wood a strong new tree.
A gift like your kingfisher, 'seldom seen',
Its bright blur arrowing from present to future.
Reminded of time, I rise to leave: you stop

> Reluctantly, though such talk must tire.
> You come to the door, invite me again, wave
> And return to living these your youngest years.[104]

The emphasis upon Clarke's link with the literary past indicates a basic attraction for Weber. Yeats fashioned Weber's way of seeing Ireland. He does not, as does Kinsella, see Yeats as essentially an English poet in the tradition of Blake, Rossetti, and Morris. For him Yeats began modern Irish verse and re-oriented poetry:

> Continue to mock the critical, fatal sages;
> When lust and Dublin drove Yeats to rages
> Eng Lit shook and dropped her pages.[105]

However, if Weber or any other contemporary poet is to build on the tradition of Yeats an anachronistic reordering of the society will have to take place.

The poems Weber writes about lust and love have little in common with Yeats's metaphoric shaping of personal experience into cultural comment. The actual presence of the people dominates, as is true of most of the contemporary writers. In "A Book of Photographs," for instance, he writes on a theme Yeats often used, the incompleteness of men, women, and love. But never does the scene, so familiar and touching, become lost in a vision of anything else. His poems about Ireland are also immediate. In "Stephen's Green Revisited" he evokes a scene that has *almost* become emblematic in Irish writing:

> The spring sun bends down between the branches.
> The ducks continue with their cry of *aqua, aqua*.[106]

Yet he quickly brings the scene into personal relevance much as did Kinsella in "Phoenix Park":

> Six months have passed since then
> And we have said goodbye again in another city.
> We have everything to hope for, yet I write sadly.
> Memory is the mother of the muses, someone said.
> But sadness is surely the secret mother of the memory.[107]

The self-conscious and effective metaphor is a technique of a writer who wants his values as well as his tradition grasped by the reader. The technique, resembling that of the confessionalist poets, tends to be rhetorical. However, such obviousness will be necessary until the tradition Weber has chosen to work in becomes strong enough again to produce emblems — if indeed that is possible now.

*Brendan*
*Kennelly*

The unlikely cooperative effort of Rudi Holzapfel, who has adopted Ireland, and Brendan Kennelly, now at Trinity, presents in a ten-year capsule the reconstruction of self, then of Irishman, from the aegis of the past. No place or person or institution is too holy for Kennelly's wit in *Cast A Cold Eye* (poems by Holzapfel and Kennelly). Even a pastoral scene turns into a consideration of woman seldom ventured by earlier writers:

> Today,
> A pied sun whimpers and shoreline trees
> Search whey-floss floozies for a lay
> In sombre storminess; the moment's bride
> Freezes on her antique frieze,
> Alabaster garments touch her knees
> And the groping fingers of the connoisseur
> Are kept from experience of the depths of her.[108]

In these poems, so much in the contemporary mode, a whimsical question is raised about the basis of liberal views in naive and youthful enthusiasm, as happens in "The Reckoning of Ptarmigan Jones," a poem about a man who sees enough to disturb the surety of his tolerance and convictions.[109]

For many of the contemporaries, and again Kavanagh comes to mind, cynical despair in the face of a country separated from the profit making and sharing world appears often, as in Kennelly's "Friend at St. Anne's":

> But Summer's dead, look at the pieces,
> I see the future covered in leases,
> Oboes tuning under the dunes,
> Tin Spoons in plastic spittoons. . . .[110]

Not only the middle class but the tinker tied to "suffering and song" and the factory girls whose lives must be as pallid as their faces are pale receive his concern.[111]

Kennelly's attacks and his association with Holzapfel make him seem at first glance to be very much the outsider. He is not. Kennelly has taken to himself several traditions which suit him quite well: the wild Irish bard, the Trinity academic, the commemorator of Ireland's cultural past. He has developed personae. His main one is Moloney, a wild rake whose life defies and destroys middle-class aplomb. Sexual forays, often with a macabre theme, typify him. He may lie with a corpse at a wake, or with a live woman on his mother's grave. Within Irish culture, according to Vivian Mercier, these poems are not at all radical but express two basic themes in Irish comedy: the macabre and grotesque.[112] The Irish, as do all people, laugh at what terrifies and mystifies them in an attempt to control themselves.

A more obvious facet of Kennelly's traditionalism is his profession and its byways. TCD, the Protestant fort of Irish academia, seems a strange place for a Catholic bard unless one considers Kennelly's serious concern with the literary heritage of Ireland. He has been assistant director of the Yeats International Summer School in Sligo and has been a frequent lecturer there. Most likely, the Yeatsian title to the first volume he and Holzapfel did together was of Kennelly's conception since his co-author dislikes Yeats. Joyce and O'Conner also concern him. In "Light Dying" he remembered O'Conner's objection to the destruction of some eighteenth-century buildings: "So you were angry at the pulling down. Of what recalled a finer age. . . ."[113] This poem has much meaning for Kennelly, as does the destruction of Georgian Dublin; for both indicate the destruction of a past that he would like to see kept alive. In another poem, "Crows," he satirizes Joyce's detractors without ever using a proper name.[114] Quite often, Kennelly sets his comment in a metaphoric structure (his term) without even making an implied comparison.[115] The result is perhaps allegory rather than metaphor. His allegorical writing seems the result of a belief in a viable ontological structure.

At the center of this structure is Dublin of the *writer*, with its stout and talk (honest talk, mind you) — and memories of Patrick Kavanagh. The complexity of Kavanagh, a visionary for some and an unpleasant parody for others, becomes in Kennelly's memory something else again:

> A man I knew who seemed to me
> The epitome of chivalry
> Was constantly misunderstood.
> The heart's dialogue with God
> Was his life's theme and he
> Explored its depths assiduously
> And without rest.[116]

The language here seems forced and rhetorical, as artificial as his portrait of Kavanagh the knight errant. Too many people remember his prejudices and unkindness to accept this view without much qualification. Even Dublin itself is cast in a somewhat misleading role, quite reminiscent of Kavanagh's characterization:

> Very soon, I'll up and take a walk
> Along a route I have not planned,
> I'll think of Dublin's treacherous talk
> And its malignant silences.[117]

This view, repeated in "Dublin: A Portrait," is an undoubtedly accurate one of a city easily classified as viciously paranoid. However, Kennelly has chosen to live there and accept, justifiably, much of its magnificence.

Kennelly, inheritor of several ironic traditions, becomes often a poet as sensitive and kind as he is deft. In "The Girl Next Door" he calls into being the life of the lonely Dubliner with an offhanded grace:

> Alarmed to life, she encounters the cold floor,
> Washes, dresses, gulps a quick cup of tea;
> A vain glance for letters there at the front door,
> Legs it through morning rain, hops the 15B.[118]

Though very evocative of Dublin, the poem touches many lives.

Even in a poem limited to mental experience, such as "Dream of a Black Fox," his attitude is unquestionably Irish. Unlike others who are concerned with specifically Irish culture, Kennelly does not re-examine the traditional past. He is one of the few poets who have allowed the premises and constructions of the days of the Literary Revival to stand without change.

*Rudi Holzapfel*

The sometimes collaboration of Kennelly and Holzapfel came about because of proximity, talent, and (one supposes) separation from the mainstream of Dublin life. Kennelly from the west and Holzapfel from America both seem drawn to an idea of Dublin that is shared, in print at least, by very few writers who are native Dubliners or grew up there. Also, a cynicism gradually assuaged by an assertion of uncontemporary values links Kennelly and Holzapfel. In *The Rain, The Moon* Holzapfel is openly censorious of what Yeats called "this filthy modern tide." Holzapfel in "Ballad of Sean the Short" writes of a man who lost his sweetheart to "that sallow man/ With his brand-new Chevrolet."[119] In "Crickets Can Sleep in the Snow" cynicism and modern references are again characteristic. They are but the patina, and the body of the poem is old-fashioned lyricism:

> Together we played in that ramshackle house
> And ate seedless grapes on the porch,
> And saw an old spider spin a new web,
> A dragonfly drunk in the dust. . . .[120]

In his more recent poems, Holzapfel's cynicism does not dominate or attempt to. The opening poem in *Translations From the English* presents the reader with a view of man rediscovered:

Before you turn the page,
However my credentials;
Two balls, one heart and half a smile —
Thems are essentials.[121]

Having described himself, with approval, in terms that would apply to many men, Holzapfel continues with a poem about an ancestor which makes the above seem rubrical:

Chew on this, comrade,
And lie awake nights . . .
400 tanks, one battleship,
2530 operational flights
With a little German Geist
And German guts.[122]

Holzapfel's poems differ from most of the ones here mentioned because his concern is with old-fashioned heroism. Such a view does not rest easily in a society that would equate all men and prescribe all belief. In *"Contra Democritatem"* he indicates his rejection of such prescription:

Glory be to the ten ton tonk
And the tripple-titted twat
For the Devil is Adolph Hitler
And God is god knows what!
                              (traditional)[123]

Calling attention to the thought processes of the Allies (or should I say democracies today) has often been done: black-white structure, sexual identification with the machine, removal of God. However, since the statement is made by contrasting the two sides of the war in Europe, quite a bit of force results that would be lacking in a more commonplace statement. In his 1967 broadside *For Love of Ireland* he can accept nation without being dominated by its concerns:

Now that the fuss is over, and the smoke has cleared and the
    sound;
Now that the flag is down and the dead of seven centuries
Can stop their awful rolling in the ground;

105

> I lay my wreath upon your tomb and break two proud German knees
> To kneel beside the dead and gone—
> A bastard, Ireland, but a bastard son![124]

However, much more than some, Holzapfel is drawn into poetic diction of a type that jars. "Heimkehr," especially because of the mixture of diction, arouses curiosity:

> How are you, Connor, *mo caofach*? and Toland, you of the meadows?
> And thou of no name — my thanks for that double at closing![125]

One is tempted to regard "thou" as ironic, except that it occurs in variant forms frequently enough to seem affected.

His attraction to the romantic patriot poet James Clarence Mangan fits well with his own Irishness. This poet is the source of the out-of-style diction found in so many of Holzapfel's poems, but the cause is in his own commitment to a romantic ideal.[126] Also he finds within the culture sanction for his own madcap adventures and whimsical verse. Known to some in Dublin as Rudi Hellsapoppin, he has used his irreverent wit to remind himself and others of the humanity of man. Perhaps he intended to remind a venerable poet of his own frailty when he quipped after Austin Clarke sold some manuscripts to the University of Texas that "Austin used to be the capital of Texas/ Now Texas is the capital of Austin."[127]

As varied and important as the Dolmen Press seems from the list of poets published there, its importance is more far-reaching yet. After *Poetry Ireland* began again, this time with John Jordan as editor, and predictably failed to gain sufficient financial support, the Dolmen kept alive the spirit of the periodical. In small volumes called *The Poetry Ireland Series*, Liam Miller publishes first volumes by young poets who show much promise. Juanita Casey, Michael Hartnett, and Richard Ryan are three in whom Miller has enough confidence to publish. Miller's influence extends even to areas in which he has no direct, editorial involvement. Richard Ryan edited a series called *Broadsheet* which is printed by the

Dolmen.[128] Dolmen poets publish there frequently, and the format recalls the tastefulness of Miller's editions. Also the Dolmen has published Denis Devlin, who is perhaps a major poet. That two volumes were published posthumously indicates Miller's willingness to correct oversights.

### CHAPTER VI

# Threshold

*Threshold* was begun in 1957 by Maire O'Malley and has continued until the present, with one significant silent period, to provide Northern Ireland with sensible criticism and responsible imaginative writing. Anywhere in Ireland, but especially in the six Northern counties, such restraint for over ten years is remarkable. In the midst of a volatile political situation and during a time of literary upheaval, *Threshold* has been neither derisive nor incendiary. Many of the writers are, however, openly liberal or radical in their beliefs, which indicates that the periodical may have to step into the street, cross its threshold of removal in the edifice of art and decorum. Though recognizing this situation, Mrs. O'Malley has attempted to avoid the factionalism that inevitably controls every periodical. The foreword to the spring/ summer issue of 1961 reads:

> The political division of Ireland, inevitably, had an influence on the development of writers in the North.[1]

With the turmoil in the North increasing, the writer will be forced into taking a stand if he realizes that his culture is not part of the Anglo-Saxon tradition but must be forged and accepted on Ulster soil. For some of the new writers, this realization will be unavoidable; but for many confusion still exists as Denis Ireland inadvertently revealed as he discussed the end of Anglo-Irish literature:

> As an Ulster Presbyterian I'm glad the road no longer exists. It does my heart good (and, incidentally, by lumping them together, also puts paid to some old Presbyterian scores!) to see my Catholic fellow countrymen not only coming into their own, but beginning to fashion an Ireland that may some day fit into the fabric of the new Europe. But I'm not so glad if it means — if it

> must mean — that the Anglo-Irish have fallen silent, for I very much doubt if
> in a foreknowable future we shall again produce a literature as brilliant as
> that which began in those Eighteenth century Protestant country house
> libraries and finally ran itself into the ground with Denis Johnston's *Moon in
> the Yellow River*.[2]

No real community exists in the North. The writers, though
calling themselves Ulstermen, automatically call to mind Southern writers when thinking about Irish literature.

*John
Hewitt*
John Hewitt's career since his early writing
in 1932 has been characterized by honesty and
respect for craft. As poetry editor of *Threshold*
he did much to effect the remarkably high level
of verse published there, and in his reviews he seriously attempted to separate what had real worth from that which lacked both
substance and craft. He has recognized the worth of John Montague and Thomas Kinsella, about whom he said: "I do not know
any other young Irish poet who shows such a grasp of form as
Thomas Kinsella at his best, and when his eye is on the object."[3]
Implicit here is Hewitt's own predilection for poetry which does
not move from objects outside the poet to conditions within the
poet. And Kinsella is one of those poets more concerned with
inner than with outer weather, a distinctly un-Northern concern.

Hewitt, though, was not unfair to Kinsella, nor was he unfair
to Patrick Kavanagh, by providing that one with a restrained yet
trenchant view. Hewitt has written the best examination of
Kavanagh's verse. While admiring his persistence in writing verse,
he cites the roughness, the lack of craft with accuracy and reserve.
And he saves his clear and pointed analysis for the end, where it
will be most effective:

> If, however, I am treating this in too serious a manner, *if Art's a kind of fun*,
> then my answer may be, in view of the clumsy *House party to celebrate the
> Destruction of the Roman Catholic Church in Ireland*, and the obscure, flat-
> footed *Paddiad* that his jokes are not good enough.[4]

This review of *Come Dance with Kitty Stobling* was needed.

In a review of Colum's *Poet's Circuits*, Hewitt placed himself
as one who prized the agrarian song, who was schooled in the

decorum of the past. He doubted if he could or would move into a brasher and unlimited part of the twentieth century. He realized that in prizing such a view, he was holding on to a tradition destined to die with him.[5]

Hewitt, as do others of his generation, believes in a literary community, separate from the rest of the community and often separate from the subject as well. Hewitt is a city man who believes the agrarian subject to be the one a poet should select. However, he begins and remains an outsider to the country people. As he often says:

> You are coarse to my sense, to my washed skin;
> I shall maybe learn to wear dung on my heel. . . .[6]

Unlike the Georgian poets he so often resembles, Hewitt does not pretend to be part of the rural scene. But unlike them, he does not often enough work with the life that is unmistakably his.

Instead, he approaches his rural experiences theoretically. Unable to abandon rural life or accept it, he develops an "understanding" predicated by past literary traditions. In "Piraeus" he calls up the Greek epics, which a well-read man would know, as a way of developing a tie between himself and someone who has not been torn from the peasants' world by cultivated life. Travelling by ship between Greek islands he sees a man marked unmistakably "farmer" and reflected in the last stanza of the last poem in his collected poems:

> Trying hard, I could not imagine
> aboard which ship in Homer's catalogue
> he might have served.[7]

The animals of the country, which so fill Hewitt's poetry that he is best known for his poems about them, very much resemble his country people.[8] In usually pleasant and exacting structures, he repeatedly tells of his unfamiliarity with the natural world. As in "A Rhyme for Blake," his structure is literary tradition. Unlike his mentors, he does not use what he views as emblematic of his own existence but as his own removal from the subject itself. In the first stanza, he presents a charmingly evocative picture of a lamb and suggests the ram to come. In the second stanza, the ram appears and the poet retreats:

> From lamb to ram, from innocence
> to the horn-proud lust that has no pretence,
> is too wide a stride for my mind to take;
>
> . . . . . . . . . . . . . . . . . . . . . . . . . . . . . . . .
>
> Did He who made the lamb make thee?[9]

No irony is intended here, and Blake's question is no longer rhetorical. Still, Hewitt chooses to find nature the alternative to society: "I have turned to the landscape because men disappoint me."[10] It is more ordered than man's world and moves by laws, though he would limit them to bloodless, lustless ones, much as did Yeats when he restructured the epic tales of primitive Ireland.

The mention of Yeats signals the appearance of the most important part of Hewitt's literary tradition. That the Literary Renaissance, like the 1916 Rebellion, was a Southern development fits Hewitt unmistakably into the dilemma of the Ulster writer, one who functions in terms of a system that has not taken him into consideration. Oisin is Hewitt's recurring example of the heroic age, that age he would see as golden. And though he can see the hero in a "flat-footed red-necked farmer," his real intent in this poem, "Homestead," is to relate Yeats to the hero: "Yeats was Oisin."[11] Yeats, too, could not bridge the gap between the country people and his own life as poet. On this separation much of Hewitt's poetry is based.

Hewitt, for all his structured ways of thought and verse, did not develop an ease with the society in which he existed. On the most important problem of his place and time, the question of what is Irish, he again imposed theoretical limits which restrict even his humanity. He remembers his own Planter background, which has caused so many of his kind to destroy the people they have displaced. But he looks at the earlier inhabitants with interest and some awe:

> The sullen Irish limping to the hills
> bore with them the enchantments and the spells
> that in the clans' free days hung gay and rich
> on every twig of every thorny hedge. . . .[12]

Closer memories than wrongs done by his ancestors plague him, as they do all men of human compassion. In "The Green Shoot," he tells how he practiced taunts he was schooled in by "bolder friends":

> In my harsh city, when a catholic priest,
> known by his collar, padded down our street,
> I'd trot beside him, pull my schoolcap off
> and fling it on the ground and stamp on it.[13]

Such training has caused many of his breed to murder, but Hewitt grew another way. His mentality identified with the Irish. In an attempt to understand their often aimless, often unkind ways, he developed a theory based on the Celtic migration that swept the people to the last corner of Europe:

> We are not native here or anywhere.
> We were the keltic wave that broke over Europe,
> and ran up this bleak beach among these stones:
> but when the tide ebbed, were left stranded here
> in crevices, and ledge-protected pools
> that have grown saltier with the drying up
> of the great common flow that kept us sweet
> with fresh cold draughts from deep down in the ocean.[14]

Essential to his theory is a longing for the mainland that drives the young to emigration and the old to anger.[15]

When confronted with facts too shocking to fit any theory, Hewitt writes beautiful and tender poems.

> This shook me once that one, a cripple child,
> loved by no mother, given another's love
> not warm with kind but aimed, deliberate,
> which, in a space of months with some expense
> of will and resolution, turned the wry bone
> in life's way straighter, should an hour unwatched
> strike a sharp death in a squalid accident,
> and all that social-love deliberate
> run twelve ways wasted in the indifferent dust:
> For I could sieve no metaphor from this
> would lift the heart against adversity.[16]

Hewitt brought by himself to confront an unpleasant fact of man and nature produces a poem much less measured than many he had written. But the force of his experience measures his art as he attempts to express and admits the limits of structure and rhetoric before existence.

In late poems he works also with a subject too factually part of his existence for the fabric of his metaphor to hold comfortably: his family. Like all families, his had antagonisms, strong leaders, intentional and accidental tendernesses. He reflects in "A Victorian Steps Out" on a day when his grandmother, Protestant of course, joined a religious procession in the street. She was not a party to the belief, but she championed the people who were being jeered at by a mob. The grand gesture, produced by an honest respect for the rights of others, was typical of this woman: "one dreadful day she told the minister his sermons never shook one sinner's heart."[17] Poems on a banished uncle and a grandfather who called his children to sing hymns as he died have the same touch of fact.[18] And in the descriptions, Hewitt presents people and actions that become universal yet do not lose their particularity.

In "The Modelled Head," by far his most introspective poem, Hewitt tells of coming to resemble his father. In a sculpture of his own head, he saw his father's face; so he is left to decide what course to follow now that he becomes his past.[19]

Hewitt's importance to Ulster poetry, and that of Ireland in general, is significant. As a critic and a poet, he did not lie or pretend — though he also had an approach rooted in a now less significant past. Probably the example of his own life affected his countrymen as much as did his writing. In several excerpts from his autobiography, published in *The Honest Ulsterman*, he tells of battles with committee men (of the Joe McCarthy kind) and of Ulster that can so swiftly turn hero into pariah simply on the basis of association. John Hewitt, agnostic in a religiously fervent land, committed in a time of compromise, rational in criticism when personal animus controls, has done much for the arts of his time and nation. If too often he refuses to consider the validity of contemporary innovation, he does not make pretence.

Roy McFadden founded *Rann*, which at-
*Roy* tempted for five years to instil a sense of com-
*McFadden* munity among Ulster writers, to produce a literature. Not only did that attempt fail to gather the poets or to affect the total community, but the poets
themselves moved with difficulty and reticence into the last half
of the twentieth century. For McFadden, the answer to the traditional absence of a community in the North is the ease with which
writers can become part of the business world, sell out:

> The pressures against creative writing are enormous. The writer who wants
> to write about his society is obliged to break away from the main flow of
> community life. He is forced to recognize that he is an odd man out, an
> outsider looking in.[20]

This sense of being an outsider, of course, touches almost every
poet in contemporary Ireland but quite differently in the South
from in the North. In the South memory of a literary community
exists to be rebelled against.

Also, as McFadden so well illustrates, the North endured
much hardship in World War II. In *A Poem. Russian Summer*, he
deals with man's putting at distance his fear of death. An illustra-
tion to the poem shows lovers in the foreground, bombers and
searchlights in the background. Even love must, in such a time, be
a distraction from fear. The war, business, religion: these are
Ulster concerns. And like the Victorians who so molded the
character of the Northern people, they want their art to entertain
and not arouse. The war itself shook poets into questioning the
permanence of any part of life, as McFadden shows in "Lines by
Slieve Donard." Understandably, when faced with present destruction, people retreat into the past. And in that past, no joy
relieved distress or encouraged the hope of a better world to
come.

Predictably, McFadden is angry. He castigates not only the
North but the South as well, which somewhat surprises, especially in comparison with John Hewitt's Anglo-Irish oriented
verse. In "The Island of Saints and Scholars," McFadden observes
the straits into which Ireland has fallen:

115

We have betrayed them one and all.
The Dublin intellectual,
The Belfast bigot, have become
The character of Irishdom.[21]

The past for him remains desirable, but he does not attempt to retreat into it. Much of his understanding of the literary community was based on Yeats and the Literary Renaissance. Though he does not speak of his removal from that community, he acknowledged the death of Yeats's aristocracy in "Letter to an Irish Novelist (*For Michael McLaverty*)" and in "Letter to London (*For Peter Wells*)."[22] Though he writes nostalgically of Swift and Yeats, he knows they are gone, taking with them the country not only of their minds but of their times; and so he is left to ask: *"Is there no country for us?"*[23] The loss of place and the absence of a center of literature, he shares with the Southern writer. Like them he also turned from the poetry of Yeats (for he had written a spiritless poem called "Cuchulain").[24] He looked towards the emergence of a new art in a revived Europe.

McFadden has recognized the need to treat experiences and people directly, without gloss; but he resembles Hewitt in having no precedent for such art. He strikes a banal tone in writing of a man killed when he wrecked his bicycle:

Maybe a girl was waiting when he was hurled
Headlong at death, when the wheel struck him, fell
And loosed the life in him.[25]

But when Roy McFadden accepts a subject worth his talent and a diction natural to a man living in the last half of the twentieth century, he can write significantly. Published in *Threshold* was "Contemplations of Mary," which presents a subject not tied to grandiose gestures of the past but based on life in his own place and time:

Now she was empty. The last drop had gone,
And she was her own Mary, uninvolved
With parables or politics, resolved
To self, undedicated, pledged to none.
And just before the colours blurred, dissolved,
She closed the door on her disfigured son.[26]

116

So much of McFadden's poetry has tried to get to this point of honest diction and emotion. That he achieved such a poem infrequently does not censure him as much as it does the literary scene within which he had to function.

As was true for Hewitt, McFadden had to continue the old belief in a literary community, one not native to his own culture. If they had not struggled to make old forms continue, who would have known the impossibility of living as had the writers of the Literary Revival?


*John*
*Montague*

John Montague first published in *The Dublin Magazine* in 1949 and then in *Envoy* in 1950, both indicating the internationalism that strongly influenced his writing.[27] Most of his volumes of poetry have come from the Dolmen Press, indicating his concern with the literary establishment of the South. For over ten years he has been associated with *Threshold* and he publishes, also, in *The Honest Ulsterman*. Increasingly in recent years, he has published or given readings in Ulster. For though Montague is a writer of international concern and wide travel, the troubles in Ulster have bothered him greatly. His most ambitious work, a long poem called *The Rough Field*, presents the pangs of Ulster in a personal and historical context. And the issue of *Threshold* he edited in 1970 attempts to open the door to the street. Perhaps, it will be as well an important opening into the future for the poets of Northern Ireland. Though Montague knows he cannot as a poet of consequence limit himself to a single province of the world, he also knows that a writer must come to an understanding with his own specific culture. In all others, especially Southern Ireland, he will remain a visitor.

Even in the early 1950's when Montague was preparing to leave Ireland for America, one of his parting remarks recognized the tie between the poet and his country, as he assessed the worth of *The Bell* for himself as a young writer:

> *The Bell* has developed an argumentative complex, and by constantly keeping in mind the social angle or problem has tended to lead writing away from its real purpose at the present time, the imaginative and honest expression of

117

> the writer's own problems, not those of his sickening community, though one will indirectly be reflected in the other.[28]

The implicit internationalist's rejection of *a country* as the fit residence for an artist does not destroy Montague's understanding that no writer leaves his culture.

Perhaps his travels in the United States brought him to see the importance of Ireland. The title of the volume which records his life at that time suggests as much: *Forms of Exile.* During his time of exile in the land in which he was born but did not accept as home, he was struck, as even Americans are, by the cheapness of much of the culture. In "American Landscapes," three poems record some of these experiences. "Bus Stop in Nevada" ties together synthetic surroundings, the greasy spoon restaurant and the slot machines, with people of misspent lives. "Hollywood and Vine" shows the parade of awkward and crude young people on the make.[29] These were reactions of a man who had not assessed his own culture, for later in "The Siege of Mullingar" he would applaud a similar crude parade as coarse but alive. In this early volume, he does recognize the entrance of a new and destructive force, though for him it at the time seems an American phenomenon.

In *A Chosen Light*, his most recent volume, Montague reflects back to the time of his visit to the United States. "All Legendary Obstacles" tells of a meeting between two lovers after a long separation:

> You had been travelling for days
> With an old lady, who marked
> A neat circle on the glass
> With her glove, to watch us
> Move into wet darkness
> Kissing, still unable to speak.[30]

This poem is based on the Orpheus and Euridice myth: the lovers are the woman and the poet who brings her back from hell; the old woman is one of the fates, who watch all that man does; and a Black porter guards the gate of hell. However, the mythic quality is not important in itself, but because of its ability to relate the "particular destiny which has been worked out" by the people in their own lives.[31]

Montague's belief that patterns exist, though implicit in his earlier poetry, becomes a major concern as he frees himself from the binding old molds of the North in particular and of Ireland in general. *Poisoned Lands* records his cynical rejection of the political and cultural lethargy that the internationalists attacked. Exile/ emigration seemed inevitable to Montague, as he indicated in a review, "Outward Bound," which he published in *Threshold* in 1960.[32]

At this time, the past of Ireland was embodied in its old people, ones who held to the past with a necrophiliac's singularity of purpose. "Like Dolmens Round My Childhood, The Old People" won first prize in the May Morton Memorial Poetry Competition sponsored by *Threshold*. Montague described that past as he then saw it living in Ireland:

> Ancient Ireland, indeed! I was reared by her bedside,
> The rune and chant, evil eye and averted head,
> Formorian fierceness of family and local feud.
> Gaunt figures of fear and friendliness,
> For years they trespassed on my dreams,
> Until once, in a standing circle of stones,
> I felt their shadows pass
>
> Into that dark permanence of ancient forms.[33]

The shedding of the pull of the old people comes to Montague, interestingly enough, in the midst of the ancient past. The appeal of this past will become, in time, for him a strength on which to build. But at this time, it simply represents a way of life he neither believed in nor wished to emulate. Montague espoused the new, non-heroic modern man. In "Old Mythologies" he asserted that the old heroes were, at last, dead.[34]

The central point of Montague's rejection in *Poisoned Lands*, however, is the Church. The importance of Jansenism in Irish Catholic thought certainly contributes to its puritanism, as does the effect of Victorian England as a shaping force of modern Ireland. In "Rome, Anno Santo," Montague contrasts the starkness of Irish Catholicism with the exuberance and beauty to be found in Italy:

> The olive-skinned impudent boys dive wildly by
> Thieving for pennies. In this splendid Italian sun
> Ranked façades proclaim a church's humanism:
> Bernini's baroque flares out in joyous ecstasy;
> But the Irish matrons, girded in nun-like black,
> Pilgrims from Georgian buildings above the slow canal,
> Or stone-fenced fields beside the Atlantic's wrack,
> March towards their God, with bead and book,
>     relentlessly.[35]

Probably, for a poet and a Catholic, references to Southern Ireland come automatically, even if he is from the North. In "Soliloquy on a Southern Strand," which was reprinted in *The Guinness Book of Poetry, 1958/59*, a priest thinks back on his youth in Ireland. He, an uncomfortable country boy, took the cloth probably because he doubted himself in a complex urban society. Now on holiday in Sydney he sees youth, exuberance, while he but suns: "Is it for this mild ending that I/ Have carried all this way my cross?"[36] These two poems, effective as they are in their censure, did not develop into even a significant theme for Montague. He observed: "'Rome, Anno Santo' and 'Soliloquy on a Southern Strand' are about nineteenth-century Irish Catholicism. The church I grew up in is not really a church at all. Those are about the wrong kinds of belief; those are about the Victorian Irish Church; but I realized afterwards that it was not really worth attacking."[37]

None of Montague's poems in *Poisoned Lands* contain this bitter rejection, though little escapes its aura. "Murphy in Manchester" by suggestion continues the castigation of an Ireland that forces its people into exile. Murphy needs work, which he finds in England. In a very commonplace image, Montague has caught the stranger's joy at seeing an object which in memory belongs to his home: "Passing a vegetable stall/ With exposed fruits, he halts./ To contemplate a knobby potato/ With excitement akin to love." He then takes Murphy to the factory where he works and the whistle which will lock him in.[38] The mixture of emotions in this poem occurs frequently in Montague's poetry as he writes of people, whom he understands, trapped by conditions over which they have no power. The Ireland of *Poisoned Lands* is barren, destroyed by lethargy and fear that have been centuries building. Yet even in these bitter or sardonic poems enters Montague's welcoming of life wherever it may be found and for as long as it may last.

*A Chosen Light* contains mature poems of a man who has, he thinks, conquered and controlled anger. Many of the poems appeared in earlier volumes. And Montague concerns himself as much with showing where his life has been, as with showing where it is, and where it may go.

World War II is part of him. As a child going to school in Northern Ireland, he saw German prisoners in barbed wire enclosures:

A small incident, soon submerged
In our own brisk, bell-dominated rule;
Until, years later, I saw another camp —
Rudshofen in the fragrant Vosges —[39]

Because he does not make a strict separation between himself and others, he became part of the humanity that was exterminated as well as part of the people who had enclosed the enemy in zoo-like cages. In describing the details of both experiences, Montague presented a ritual of confinement that debases and destroys humanity.

It is this memory of World War II that often informs the poetry of John Montague in a way that has scant reference in the poetry of Southern Ireland. This memory in the above poem becomes amplified by another as both are set into a series that recalls the war years in his memory of the past and his re-experience of the past. In "Vigil" he tells of feeling again the threat of danger present in Northern Ireland during the War. As the air raid sirens are tested in Paris long after the War, he describes the separation between Northern and Southern Ireland:

> That is the real border, the grit
> Of different experience, of shared terror
> No swift neutral sympathy can allay.
> Only the rising pulse of the All Clear
> Cleanses, permits the day.[40]

Reference to the "border" calls up another cage experience which will become increasingly important in Montague's poetry: the separation of the two Irelands by a rebellion that excluded the North.

In *A Chosen Light* he is a man working out an understanding of the powers which direct him. In a series of three poems, called "A Chosen Light," Montague tells of memories and images that confine him. The poem, "11 rue Daguerre," describes the atelier in Paris where he lives. At the time the poem was written, this was his chosen light, where he would live and write, the one place most suited to the ritual he felt compelled to acknowledge. As is true of all human experience, life here lacks undivided joy. The sight of a school master with children in Luxembourg takes him on a voyage inside that "handsome hawklike head," calling to mind the cages which destructively confine. Again, seeing some radiometers, Montague follows the image. Filling it out with present details, he constructs a like one on the desk of an executive or by his mistress's bed as it casts its light:

> Over unhappiness, ceaselessly
> Elaborating its signals
> Not of help, but of neutral energy.[41]

All in society seems to be waiting for an answer. The answer which Montague offers is love based on an understanding of humanity and on the phenomena of love.

Love, too, encloses people by directing their actions. In "A Charm" Montague describes the love which binds man and woman as producing both pleasure and pain as he relates man and woman to falcon and falconer:

> But how my talons
> Ache for the knob
> Of your wrist![42]

Like the bird, man finds the hood and wrist more compelling than limitlessness. But the woman must protect herself from the fact of pain that is part of all wild things.

In dealing with experiences predicated by customs he respects or which are too unsettling to fit analogies, Montague creates such details that necessitate an immediate reaction. In "The Answer" he presents himself leaving a car to ask directions to Gallarus. The old woman to whom he addresses his question first responds in Irish with "the ritual greeting": "God (Mary and Patrick) to you." Stepping momentarily into a way of life rapidly disappearing from the contemporary, impersonal world, he feels she has invoked "powers/ to cleanse the mind." Implicit in the poem is Montague's recognition of Irish custom as able to produce a way of life that has both grace and affection. He often describes old women with details which lead to understanding the ritual of their lives, the customs that have come to determine their mannerisms, and the accumulated experience that has produced their understanding. In "Paris, April 1961," about the Algerian Putsch, another old woman appears, selling newspapers:

> And when I asked the woman at the kiosk
> 'Il y a quelque chose de nouveau?'
> She said: 'C'est tout dans le journal.'
> She probably said that before the *Blitzkrieg*.[43]

She is another of the fates who looks upon the passing scene, recognizing that man once again performs his universal acts.

Through the eyes of old women, Montague often shows the patterns, or rituals, of existence which lead to peace of mind.

In "The Wild Dog Rose," written as part of *The Rough Field*, Montague tells how he finally overcame the last trace of fear in himself of an old woman who had terrified him as a child. Thought to be a hag, *cailleach* in Irish, she lived a solitary life because she was avoided by all. He recreates in the opening of the poem the old fear he felt in approaching this woman, who had long before become a friend:

> And I feel again
> that ancient awe, the terror of a child
> before the great hooked nose, the cheeks

dewlapped with dirt, the staring blue
of the sunken eyes, the mottled claws
clutching a stick.[44]

As they sit chatting, Montague finds as she rehearses "the small
events of her life," an understanding that binds his and all others'
understanding to the fact of her life:

The only true madness is loneliness,
the monotonous voice in the skull
that never stops
                        because never heard.[45]

The ritual of loneliness necessitates talk of a most personal nature
when two friends meet, as happens here. She tells of her rape by a
drunk and of her praying to Mary, another virgin, for help. The
poem leads away from the poet's self and into the merger of Mary,
old woman, wild rose with the suggestion that suffering and
loneliness exist in all lives.

In "The Hag of Beare," Montague translates a poem by one
of the early Irish women poets. In his discussion of the poem,
Montague explains both his concern with the hag and his attraction to early Irish life. She is another Kali, only here cast into a
time struggling "between paganism and Christianity, between
worldly pleasure and the doctrine of salvation through repent-
ance."[46] She is the only one of Montague's old women who has
been shaped by active and passionate life.

In her rituals, the hag did not so much struggle against
Christianity as find some referent in it to her own life:

So God be praised
That I misspent my days
For whether the plunge be bold
Or timid, the blood runs cold.[47]

And Christ too finds himself unusually invoked; as she remembers the men who loved her and have died:

Well might the Son of Mary
Take *their* place under my roof-tree

For if I lack other hospitality
I never say 'No' to anybody.[48]

Seen in the context of his poetic intention, this poem conveys Montague's attempt to take man (especially himself) beyond the limits imposed by Britain by returning to a life more ancient than the one which developed in conquered Ireland. Implicit here, again, is condemnation of the puritanical morality that has developed in Ireland with the strong encouragement of Victorian England.

The replacement of this ancient culture by a Christian one again occupies Montague in *The Bread God*. This poem, part of *The Rough Field*, presents the effect of Cromwell on religious life in Ulster. However, as important here is an examination and censure of the state of Christianity with Northern Ireland as the medium for the general statement. Much of the conflict between Catholics and Protestants in the North has irrationally concerned holy communion. Montague would take his readers in *The Bread God* beyond topical concerns: Behind Christianity is "The original meaning of the death of the year and the Easter Ritual."[49] Christianity and the pagan past can, then, be united in a ritual which encourages love by making man a participant in the life of the earth and its seasons.

Montague conveys this possibility through the details of Catholic worship, which is the traditional church of ancient Ireland. In contrast to this belief, he puts the Protestant militants of Ulster. Casting the whole poem in a very contemporary structure of a worship service by radio, Montague begins with a note indicating a condition of disturbance:

Listeners are warned
that reception may be interfered
with by pirate stations, but every effort
will be made to provide undisturbed
contemplation.[50]

The poem proceeds with a mixture of types of information: Carleton's description of Christmas service, Montague's recreation of the service, and a priest's letter to a nephew about his vocation.

In general, for Montague, religion has lost its tie with the worship of the union between man and the earth. People have even lost love and respect for the immediate signs of their faith, as is illustrated by the inattention of a latecomer to church:

> On St. Joseph's
> Outstretched arm, he hangs his cap
> Then spends a very pleasant mass
> Studying the wen-marked heads
> Of his neighbours, or gouging
> His name in the soft wood
> Of the choirloft, with the cross
> Of his rosary beads.[51]

This inattentive man, so representative, bears little resemblance to the monster Roman Catholic of Protestant propaganda.

Periodically, announcements of Protestant fanaticism interrupt to contrast their view of the Catholic with the pictures of a quiet peasantry Montague has presented. These are frightening in themselves, but in contrast to a belief that is, at its worst, innocuous, they become statements indicative of a dangerous degree of neurosis:

> LOYALISTS REMEMBER!
> MILLIONS *have been* MURDERED *for refusing to* GROVEL
> *Before Rome's Mass-Idol:* THE HOST!
> *King Charles I and his Frog Queen Henrietta* GLOAT *in their letters*
> *that they have almost* EXTERMINATED THE PROTESTANTS OF IRELAND
> *The* PRIESTS *in every* PARISH *were told to record* HOW MANY *killed!*
> *Under* ROGER MORE AND SIR PHELIM O'NEIL
> *Instruments of* ROME
> 40,000 *loyal protestants were* MASSACRED *like game-fowl*
> IN ONE NIGHT

> '*Cromwell went to Ireland*
> TO STOP
> *The Catholics murdering Protestants!*'[52]

He began with a view of sincere worship in the past and ends with a prophecy of unity among the peoples of Ulster that depends on their comprehending the mutual bases of belief if the doctrine of love is to become important in Christian worship at the present time. The final section of *The Bread God* takes its form from French surrealist poetry and poses paradoxes which are solved by being cast into inconsequence:

> I saw the Pope carding tow on Friday
> A blind parson sewing a Patchwork quilt/
> Three bishops cutting rushes with their croziers/
> Roaring Meg firing Rosary beads for cannonballs
> Corks in boats afloat on the summit of the Sperrins/
> A mill and a forge on the back of a cuckoo/
> The fox sitting conceitedly at a window chewing tobacco/
> And a moorhen in flight
> surveying
> a United Ireland.[53]

The moorhen in flight does not see a divided Ireland, for the border and the religious conflicts exist only within people's minds. The hope offered by this view of unity, the only one in the poem, depends upon an abandonment of hostilities as unnatural. Montague is not, however, presenting a naive solution to a complex problem, as is evident in the dissonant body of the poem and in his own summary of the poem as reflecting the Protestant-Catholic conflict:

> The extreme Protestants are marching where they shouldn't, and the extreme Catholics are getting more and more extreme so that there is no possible meeting ground and there isn't in the poem except from the outside and from the passage at the end, "The Ulster Prophecy."[54]

The moorhen, so closely associated with the Irish countryside, also is associated by Montague with himself in exile. Being separate from (above) the embattled factions, he can see the spectrum as a progression of people which should complement one another, not clash. Even a poem with such topical concern as *The Bread God* has a basis in the wider experience of Ireland and of mankind.

In *Hymn to the New Omagh Road*, another section of *The*

*Rough Field*, Montague presents another of Ulster's problems, the destructiveness of the machine-age world. The poem contrasts the beauties of the land with the minimal economic value of building a road and so destroying a countryside that many have loved and written about. On such a note, the poem begins:

> As the bull-dozer bites into the tree-ringed hillfort
> Its grapnel jaws lift the mouse, the flower,
> With equal attention, and the plaited twigs
> And clay of the bird's nest, shaken by the traffic,
> Falls from a crevice under the bridge
> Into the slow-flowing mud-choked stream
> Below the quarry, where the mountain trout
> turns up its pale belly to die.[55]

The desire to control the earth, bend it to the will of man, takes many forms; but ultimately all destroy the balance of the world, perhaps of the universe.

Montague is a poet for whom satire and censure have only incidental importance. His strength is in his ability to recreate customs, rituals, and details that bind people together in love. However, the problems in the North increasingly occupy his art. His concern for his people has such importance that he turns his art to what can help his people. In *A New Siege*, a recent part of *The Rough Field*, he presents the current Protestant-Catholic struggle in the North as a repeating pattern of behavior that binds people to a destructive ritual.

The dedication of the poem indicates immediately Montague's point of view:

> for Bernadette Devlin
> Old moulds are broken in the north[56]

In the prose passage which opens the poem, Montague refers to the most immediate open conflict that broke Ireland into armed camps: the Troubles. But the remainder of his poem sets into parallel with the present the times when Ulster has tried to solve its problems with violence. Though references to Ulster's angry heroes, such as Cuchulain, enter the poem, Montague rightly begins the poem with a description of the Jacobite war:

Lines of history
      lines of power
the long sweep
      of the Bogside
under the walls
      up to Creggan
the black muzzle
      of Roaring Meg
staring dead on
      the new Cathedral
the jackel shapes
      of James' army
watching the city
      stiffen in siege.[57]

Montague identifies history and power as indistinguishable from one another in terms of the conflict that has set Ulster into patterns (molds) that must be broken if a new, invigorating life is to enter. While the leaders and their special groups of killers throw a country into conflict, the ordinary citizen loses all right to live, even to avoid starvation.

Being aware of the destructive ritual of religious conflict as well as of the joy that should be the concern of the young now, Montague begins in the middle of this poem to show the possibility of an alternative among the young. The "guardian" of an empty church that is darkened during the siege voices a rejection of present violence that must be in the minds of many. He sees no promise of peace in violence and believes the young, as well, want joy and love. The young thrown in "lines of change" across Berkeley, Berlin, Paris, Chicago also act out of accord with their immediate past. Perhaps they do, as Montague says, invoke "the new/ Christ avatar."[58] Certainly in his poems about ancient Ireland, such as "The Hag of Beare," he has shown that Christianity need not simply arouse man to destroy anyone who differs from him in race or religion.

*Tides*, completed in book form before *The Rough Field*, is a later work continuing examination of life between the polarities of unique example and form become conception. As he had seen modern history forming into "lines of power," now he sees individual lives breaking the molds of past conceptions. Somewhat like Kinsella, Montague finds the struggle between permanent forms and the necessity of destruction irreconcilable with a conception of man as an essentially purposeful being.

Two of the long poems in *Tides*, "The Wild Dog Rose" and "The Hag of Beare," more resemble the poems of *The Rough Field* than they do the starker poems with which they appear. *Tides* begins with "Premonition," which tells again of Montague's obsessive dream of the carving up of a woman's body.[59] This concern with destruction is repeated in two prose passages, especially in "Coming Events," which describes a man being flayed alive by a quite elegant and self-concerned man.[60] The ominous title finds fulfillment in a feminine counterpart. In "The Pale Light" his muse appears as a sexual experience that is awry. As Medusa, her genitals have been moved to her head; and she introduces death:

> Tears away all
> I had so carefully built —
> Position, marriage, fame —
> As heavily she glides towards me
> Rehearsing the letters of my name
>     As if tracing them from
>     A rain streaked stone.[61]

The pun in "Rehearsing" stresses the destruction, but in the pale light of morning he can see his intercourse with Medusa as the sign of death being born. In "Life Class" again the security of preconception disappears as the fact of experience is perceived. The nude model in the class appears in many roles to the people who know her and see her, varying from anatomical study for students to "hell's gaping/vaginal mouth" for the "desert fathers." In actuality, the woman-mother-wife-whatever exists in terms unable to be restrained to any or all of the conceptions.[62]

After some poems on personal losses and experiences, Montague opens *Tides* to its widest with "Sea Changes," the last section. Preconceptions gone, he sees in the ocean and its inhabitants, including man, a complex and unifying pattern. All experience passes from life to death and into life again. Forms change, but the patterns continue over which man has no control. Man

does, however, continue to trust the conceptions to which per-
ceptions lead him, knowing

> . . . there is no sea
> it is all a dream
> there is no sea
> except in the tangle
> of our minds:
> the wine dark
> sea of history
> on which we all turn
> turn and thresh
> and disappear.[63]

In his collection of short stories, *Death of a Chieftain*, Montague examined the atrophying patterns of Northern Ireland,
sometimes by looking at the people who stayed there and sometimes by tracing the paths of those who attempted exile.[64] Increasingly, however, he turns from the effect of the immediate past to
the rejuvenation that seems to be occurring among the young. In
writing for *The Honest Ulsterman*, Montague has identified himself with the people who are at least sympathetic with the radical
movement of the young. Unfortunately, as Montague has recognized in *A New Siege*, change may not occur unless it begins in the
street. And as he said in his foreward to the issue of *Threshold* he
edited, "For the time being to be an Ulster writer is, in a sense, to
be a revolutionary writer; old molds are broken in the North."[65]
In this issue, he attempted to lift the latch on the door that has
kept *Threshold* out of the street. The pieces printed, though
varied, so often began with recognizing that violence in the North
has become a central part of Christian belief. Brian Moore
watches a news report in the United States and sees thirty years
disappear as once again the wheel turns, now coming full circle as
an English soldier with gun at the ready walks through Belfast.[66]
Eoin Sweeney describes a non-violent march he and some others
made across the province — and the violence that erupted around
them among people who cannot accept peace.[67] Montague published his *A New Siege* here and Kinsella "The Pangs of Ulster,"
which goes back into epic to examine the origins of Ulster's
violence.[68]

That Montague's political statements have effect is evidenced by reference to him in a speech made by the Taoiseach, head of the government of the Republic of Ireland, Mr. Lynch:

The Irish poet, John Montague, from County Tyrone, says:
'Old moulds are broken in the North.'
We stand on the brink of a great achievement. There are those who would stop us — on both sides of the Border.

Mr. Lynch, much as Montague has done in *The Rough Field*, observed that the Irish are one people, who should not be divided by bigotry.[69]

For John Montague, an internationalist of the fifties, to be quoted in a pro-Irish speech by an official of the government indicates much about the change within the country as well as that in the poetry of Montague. For the North, at least, *Threshold* has monitored the change, which has been understandably accelerated as the seventies began. Much of the new temper of the periodical, of course, is reflected in the guest editors chosen. Seamus Heaney edited the issue before Montague's, at which time *Threshold* passed its twenty-first year and "came of age." Heaney's inclusion of new writers such as Michael Longley and Derek Mahon, and even newer writers such as Paul Muldoon and Elizabeth Walsh, shows concern with the emerging culture.[70] *Threshold*, then, may have looked into the street.

### CHAPTER VII

# The Honest Ulsterman and Atlantis

*The Honest Ulsterman: Monthly Handbook for a Revolution* obviously purports to be a radical force in Northern Ireland. However, the ethics and the politics are the socialist-liberal ones that have characterized members of the intelligentsia for most of this century. Seen within the context of Irish society, especially the Northern, *The Honest Ulsterman* represents quite well attitudes which characterize the liberal-radical contingent of the late sixties. Generally, this group is simply called The Movement indicating a uniformity of taste, ethics, politics. Often, for these people, the use of drugs and an insistence that they be allowed to structure sexual lives the establishment rejects are major concerns. James Simmons, first editor and continuing force of *The Honest Ulsterman*, attends to such concerns. But he does so without the abandon which characterizes many of his English and American contemporaries.

*James Simmons*

*The Honest Ulsterman* understandably publishes in the main young poets who have not been recognized by the prestigious publishers. Bill Turner, Michael Stephens, Michael Foley, and Frank Ormsby have frequently contributed work and have served as editors. But James Simmons, though no longer editor, has shaped the direction of the periodical. John Hewitt has often been published here, but he is the only established poet of Northern Ireland to form a close association. Seamus Heaney, Derek Mahon, John Montague, in that order, have from time to time been approved of by the editors; but none of these poets has strictly identified himself with the group.

Simmons expresses a belief that Ulster and Southern Ireland exist apart, with different problems. But Southern Irish and English publishers still control the reputations of Irish writers, as Simmons admits in reviewing a book by Patrick Boyle that Mac-Gibbon & Kee published: "There is no doubt about it that these publishers do a lovely job, and with Kavanagh, Montague, Hewitt, etc. on their list they must be the leading publishers of Irish writing."[1] Part of the reason for his concerted opposition to outside control may be that he has committed himself to living and writing in the North, accepting his separation from the South as real.

In printing and replying to a letter sent in by a radical reader, Simmons revealed a susceptibility to provocation and a moderate's adherence to existing forms of thought:

> "LIVE UP TO YOUR NAME AND PRINT THIS
> YOU BOURGEOIS-LIBERAL BASTARDS."
> signed "Cadres of the United People's Union."
>
> What followed was not quite funny enough to be satire, so I am presuming it was written seriously, and of course I know very well that a lot of serious people do talk jargon.
>
> I find it ugly and frightening, dripping with hate; but I read it carefully. I thought of printing it; but presumed that people who read this magazine have a sort of respect for language that would make them give up after the first long sentence.[2]

The summary of the letter and Simmons's analysis show it to be the work of a man either confusedly radical or highly neurotic. Working with the Marxian idea of revolution to polarize classes and with the unhealthiness of a consumer society, the writer lays all blame on a "world monetary conspiracy of Jewish bankers and C.I.A. backed tycoons."[3] Ulster is in danger, so much so that printing this letter may have been a mistake which could encourage other such people and let loose even more blood. But Simmons's reaction to the letter sounds much like that of an American liberal accused of prejudice by a Black revolutionary: "Some of my best friends are Czechoslovakian and Hungarian communists. . . ."[4] Simmons proposes an answer to the violence: the exercise of respect and reason. To this is added the expected cure of the sixties: "if we can use the artists in our midst and in ourselves, love IS all we need."[5]

*The Honest Ulsterman* does seem unusually provincial though and with good reason. At first, the coterie-like editorial group seems to be the cause, then the continuing presence of Simmons. Ulster itself, instead, causes this quality in the periodical. Real problems, ones too serious to be masked with sophisticated word play, exist in the community. Writers must deal openly and blatantly with them or seem guilty of effete withdrawal from life itself. But sincerity and concern in themselves provide little artistic merit. Simmons's "Elegy for J. F. Kennedy" illustrates the danger:

He came to Dallas, following his mission.
Bang! A bullet cured healthy ambition.
He was planning his next gesture: to kiss
His hand to a child, maybe. Then this.
Rushed, in the hands of minions, a president can't
Die with the dignity of Orwell's elephant.
The fragile man-machine was quickly broken
Too badly for last words to be spoken.
No inspiration can by-pass the fact
That speech requires a respiratory tract.[6]

Much too obviously Simmons presents an attitude certain to find approval from establishment-oriented liberals. Yet at the same time his no-nonsense or sentimental language will interest more politically excessive readers. A prefabricated poem results, well illustrating the danger of the conversational approach so characteristic of contemporary Irish poetry.

The poems in his first volume, *Ballad of a Marriage*, continue the same attitudes with obviously contemporary diction. All of the poems here, however, treat the difficulties of satisfactory love in the sexually liberated present. Writing of a husband and wife, Simmons's male narrator wonders:

When she stirred under me I saw her
Squirming in delight
In other people's cars and beds,
And sitting up all night
Her face drained white in love's despair
Because some man had not been there.[7]

135

That this situation concerns Simmons is illustrated by his return to the same theme later. The residue of an earlier morality which decreed all women should be virgins until married clearly informs Simmons's approach to life and love. Perhaps for that reason, the men in his poems appear more at ease with women they can accept on a purely casual basis. In "A Good Thing" he recounts how easily and insincerely "I love you" can be said.[8] Other poems in the volume reiterate this pronouncement of freedom and show as well the poet's inability to avoid reference to moral structures he cannot live by.

*Late But in Earnest*, Simmons's second volume of verse, contains many of the same weaknesses that spoil poems written specifically for *The Honest Ulsterman*: too great a casualness in form and diction, too much catering to his own whim. These weaknesses, however, occur mainly in long poems, which require much discipline if they are to avoid being flaccid. The two long poems in this volume are elegiac. "Elegy" works within a Roman Catholic structure and resists the entry of a reader not of the faith; for the words are signs of a particular belief, not signs of a condition all men know:

It is strange how today
A conception can, like a candle,
Be lit, and I believe
What I heard often and laughed at, see,
In the tidy huts of a settlement,
Heaven, and know Christ well enough
To trust his promise of accommodation.[9]

Soothing though such an observation may be to a family, it does not pull a reader to sympathy unless he shares the exact experience.

In his other long poem, "Dangerous Bathing," Simmons tells of a young boy who ignored a warning sign at a swimming place, perhaps thinking he was just rebelling from one more adult view of life. To attack a repressive society has been Simmons's constant concern, yet here he so begins and then turns to moralizing:

'God didn't *punish* him,' his wife
Says desperately, 'That's not what's meant . . .

> But can God think so little of a life?
> Does He let children die by accident?'[10]

The rationalizing of the parents and Simmons's own admonition to hold to "love and poetry" may well be wise, but they are both discursive observations, proceeding from a system that is neither explained nor made important in the poem.

In many of the shorter poems Simmons identifies his subjects as specifically as in the two longer ones, yet communicates tension, passion, whatever feeling is called for. Especially in his love poems he finds subjects universal and immediate. In "Husband to Wife" he moves into the confessionalist's approach with ease. As he writes his thoughts, he does so for the widest possible audience, all people who try to accept the difficulties of love and sex, without harming themselves or others. He imagines his wife before their meeting, before their marriage being sexually intimate with another man. His reaction is surprising in a poet who deals so openly with sexual conditions:

> Such thoughts have made me sweat
> And wrestle, hours, no years, against my pride;
> And to be honest, I am wrestling yet.[11]

The conversational diction, highlighted by sensual imagery, moves in rhythms that do not startle. The subject itself is unsettling enough; a more rhythmic pattern would detract from what is said.

One of his most successful poems is "Experience," and the subject, Belfast, is one he obviously paid much to learn well. He meets a man in the lavatory of a pub, who in his Belfast accent simply says, "I want to fight you." The poem does not become another accounting of the harshness of Ulster, though that exists. Instead, the reader becomes part of thudding fists that have bruised and cut innumerable bodies made into a new experience by Simmons's re-creation of what he did and felt:

> A torn shirt and my lip numb and bloody,
> My anger and — strange — the feel of my own body
> New to me, as I struck, as he struck.[12]

Simmons turns a provincial fight into a quite human experience.

Michael Stephens, who has been a guest editor of *The Honest Ulsterman*, represents quite well the new attitudes. His identification with "the movement" indicates he is of the young who assert their moral involvement in society. In "Jokes," which he published in the first issue of *The Honest Ulsterman*, a familiar theme spirited by fresh enthusiasm and a reasonably open language suggests both Stephens's youth and talent.[13]

The five poems Stephens published in this issue all reveal a similar concern with the effects of contemporary mass culture, which increasingly induces acceptance of a simplistic and artificial identity:

A cardboard Kodak Girl
Looks fixedly at me
As I walk towards her
She smiles
The same dazzling smile
As yesterday
And the day before[14]

In continuing the poem, Stephens develops his sense of separation from the other people on the street as well as from the artificiality of the adman's world.

In the next issue, he published a poem explaining even more the difference between himself and much of the world. The sound of Liverpool seems present in the sense of terminal life and the songlike conversation:

Turn me off a final time,
Let me see the end;
Don't bother with a funeral,
I haven't any friends.[15]

In this poem through the persona of Bill the Burglar, an outcast similar to many occurring in ballads and jokes, Stephens enters into fantasy, as he does repeatedly. In "Michael the Menace," for instance, he describes his aunt who is standing on a table "With her finger stuck in the light socket":

Her hair was standing up in spikes,
Her teeth were bared in a hideous grin,
And a bright glowing light
Suffused her body.[16]

Within "the movement" a hard concern with inequality and persecution is complemented by belief that anything can happen because so much seems possible. Understandably, fantasy becomes a popular mode; for in it everything does happen. Within the escape-personae of these two poems, Stephens has the two sides.

The April 1969 issue of *The Honest Ulsterman* was edited by Stephens and shows his concern with current, and often important, conditions in contemporary culture. He reviews Eldridge Cleaver's *Soul on Ice* and refers familiarly to Frank Zappa and Malcolm X, certainly three cynosures of concern among the hip. This issue has other significance to the community of Northern Ireland than news from the outside can possibly convey. An announcement early in the issue suggests a problem that everyone needs to remember is a possibility anywhere:

> There should also have been three poems by John Chadbon, but intimidation on our printers by the police (just doing our job) meant that we had to cut them out.
>
> Also missing (courtesy of Ulster's unofficial Censor) a poem by Richard Brautigan and A Thought for the Month quoted from William Burroughs.[17]

The forced exclusion of these items may well be as important as much that Stephens published. He intended to reveal Ulster's problems in this issue, and an extremely limiting practice of censorship is a significant problem.

In Stephens's issue, the concretist poetry by M. Wilkins adds variety to the familiar looking poetry published in *The Honest Ulsterman*. As startling, though, is Pete Morgan's poem about a raid that lasted all night:

PC Frog from Tipperary
hooked on God but never on Mary
banged on the table
    demanded a raid

139

> banged on the table
>     and the raid was made.[18]

The thumping rhythm, so reminiscent of Sitwell's *The Congo*, stresses the impassioned and irrational violence of Protestant Ulster, which has found a like reaction from the Catholic minority. This poem, characteristic of the ones Stephens selected for this issue, does not remove the reader from the crises of culture and life itself by a deft move into verbal patterns or morbid revelations of a disturbed being. Ulster's problems are so basic that the more direct treatment of forceful verse seems preferable. To ignore artistic innovations would, though, encourage the insularity of Ulster, and Stephens does well to present the new forms in art along with the new sounds of social protest.

In his own poetry Stephens seems more concerned with an understanding of man's psyche in contemporary terms than he is with the experimental forms of contemporary poetry. His one attempt at unconventional verse to be published in *The Honest Ulsterman* was "Birthday":

> i will
> unwrap one layer
> of my present
> the most exciting present
> Till one present day
> iwillunwrapthe present[19]

Understandably, Stephens did not reprint this poem in his booklet, *Blues for Chocolate Doherty*. The poem, existing only for its appearance, fails to lead the reader to any startling understanding. The form is already trite and, in this particular example, unable even to arouse interest in the subject. Quite possibly, Ulster and Ireland in general produce poets who cannot achieve isolation from themes and forms of wide and immediate social relevance. In England and America, poets can often separate themselves from a conscious concern with an identity dependent on their culture, sometimes become Mid-Atlantic, but more often just are writers not tied to a specific culture. For the Irish writer a total escape from the culture that produced him often results in irrelevance.

*Michael*
*Foley*

Michael Foley was guest editor of the May 1969 issue of *The Honest Ulsterman* and now with Frank Ormsby edits it. Under their direction, the periodical will continue in the way established by Simmons. Attention will be given to younger poets, and editorial views will be liberal but not radical. When he was guest editor, Foley indicated his political caution in a story, "The Revolutionaries." In it, young people assume varying radical roles, all of which are insincere. After a farcical demonstration, which shows the leaders strongly motivated by self-interest, they link arms and join in the ultimate cliche: singing "The Internationale."[20] Foley's editorial, called "Ulster Diary," echoes caution:

> I take a stroll through the Bogside. DERRY-BORN EDITOR TOURS RIOT-TORN CITY flashes through my mind and I also consider how I would make my T.V. documentary, stopping to chat up wrinkled characters and so forth. But it's not the same as the old days. How brief and tawdry glamour is, that we should no longer be excited at being the main item on the main B.B.C. News. Post revolution lethargy.[21]

By pointing out the motive of personal gain and aggrandizement in many of the people, including himself, who are active in the civil rights struggle in Ulster, Foley reminds his readers that even people involved in a heroic activity are still human. This insistence on accepting what people are, rather than seeing them as limited by principle as are tragic heroes, constitutes a major theme in contemporary Irish writing. Hopefully, this awareness in the North will prevent the revolution there, when it ends, from producing the atrophy that incapacitated the South, whose leaders were presented as demigods by their followers and by themselves.

Realization of flawed man and flawed rebellion form Foley's main theme, and it is one which gives his poetry specific direction in diction and tone. In "Grianan" he works within these limits and at the same time reflects on the Irish past: with its "hairy druids, Viking raiders, and pagan banquets." This "brutal pagan force" excites envy in him because he considers life since then to be lesser. He sees them:

> Untainted yet by scholar saints and such:
> And wonder could they possibly have bred us
> Into this, the mothers and the priests,
> The quantities of Guinness and the sloth
> The only wish a life of beautiful half sleep
> Haunted by old songs and memories of botched revolu-
> tions.[22]

Modern Ireland seldom becomes his specific concern in poems. In "Heil Hitler," he remembers "When Hitler Coyle broke into school/ And shit upon the teacher's desk." Foley's own reaction to this errant schoolboy's indecency was the same as to the crusty pagans:

> I thought it funny, even brave,
> But didn't say. I lack conviction,
> Taught this timid reasonable touch,
> Castrated early on by education.[23]

Caught as he is in personal reticence and a desire for the exercise of power, Foley reflects the dilemma of his country and suggests the danger that has been shown in Ulster rioting and violence: the past can no longer direct present action, but violence is still the ultimate answer for most people.

Foley does best when writing verse that is meditative and cautiously censorious or when commenting on the present scene so that many may proceed in his ways with some cognizance of his flaws. These are admirable traits in an editor; but risky ones in a poet, who must touch the force of human desire or aspiration. Frank Ormsby's concern with rural Ireland adds needed breadth of concern to the periodical. "Loughside" takes a reader into the country, but again problems with diction distract:

> Rush-tufted, pitted and sogged with holes.
> Caught in conspiracies of mud and liquid
> The fence posts totter there, limp in the water
> Leg by crooked leg. That day we lacked
> Patience to pick our steps. We faced around,
> Climbed with the hill farms to firm ground.[24]

If "conspiracies" and "totter" helped elucidate the use of each other, they would be important in the poem. Instead, they are only in the poem. Ormsby, also, recognizes that being a poet separates him from the mass; but unlike Foley, he doesn't turn from direct confrontation with the opposition:

> 'Ormsby's a cissy, boys, he writes poems.
> Birds and flowers, you know, and dung like that.'
> His thick eyes rolled, two sneering domes
> Set in his skull, and his loose mouth spat
> Aggressively. Around us the crowd grew,
> Mustered like vultures in the grey stone yard,
> Sniggering. What could a poet do?
>
> I flattened the big bastard.[25]

Looking at violence from different perspectives indicates a difference in cultural awareness as well as personal commitment. Perhaps the existence of two editors will keep *The Honest Ulsterman* from egocentricity in taste, a trait often appearing before.

*Seamus Heaney*     The most important poets of Northern Ireland have not been intimately associated with *The Honest Ulsterman*, though they have often found approval in it. John Montague has published poems there; his largest selection is also his most recent.[26] Of the Northern Irish poets Seamus Heaney, though, has received the most praise: "Since Seamus Heaney seems to be the best known Irish poet now writing, we invite poems in the Heaney manner on any subject to be judged by Seamus himself. First prize £1."[27] Quite likely, this note is a joke limited to the immediate family of *The Honest Ulsterman*, since the previous month's competition was on a textual matter in Graham Greene's *The Comedians* and was won by the author.

In "Writer at Work," a brief statement of process, Heaney cited Patrick Kavanagh: "Some poems one hoards like a miser for weeks in what Patrick Kavanagh might call the 'fog of unknowing', reluctant to force them into language in case the language does not measure up; others may only begin to grow under the pen, so to speak."[28] The analysis of method is of less interest than Heaney's mention of Kavanagh as precedent. Much of Heaney's poetry, as is often true for the group consistently publishing in *The Honest Ulsterman*, resembles the get-tough, no-nonsense poetry that Kavanagh presented to his reading public as honest comment upon the world. Also, the Northern poets resemble Kavanagh in concern with the real, the distinctive Irish experience. Often Seamus Heaney so isolates his subjects in their specific locale that they can be in no one else's. The compulsion or desire of an Ulster poet to capture the forms of his own existence and to accept them is often paid for dearly. In "The Early Purges" Heaney tells of his acceptance of death, that of small animals at least:

> Still, living displaces false sentiments
> And now, when shrill pups are prodded to drown
> I just shrug, 'Bloody pups'. It makes sense:
>
> 'Prevention of cruelty' talk cuts ice in town
> Where they consider death unnatural,
> But on well-run farms pests have to be kept down.[29]

Exactly what relevance pups have to men remains unclear in this one poem, taken by itself. Later, Heaney repeats his acceptance of this "businesslike" vitality in a poem about breeding a cow. These poems, taken alone, are locked in themselves, not allowed to escape into the reader. But in these poems resides much of Ulster, which holds and prizes its own, looks with pride on the struggle of its people.

A much more complex understanding of Heaney's poetry emerges when the poems are read as contiguous in statement. In "Death of a Naturalist" he remembers the contrast between a lecture in school on the mating of frogs and his first viewing of actual mating. His understanding that man and the rest of the natural world are bound together is expressed through a boyhood trauma, the sight of huge frogs:

> I sickened, turned, and ran. The great slime kings
> Were gathered there for vengeance and I knew
> That if I dipped my hand the spawn would clutch it.[30]

Heaney's understanding of the nexus between all living things seems based on a harsh rejection of animality, even a fear of being pulled into organic existence. In "Turkeys Observed" he almost shudders at the sight of plucked, chilled turkeys.[31] Implicit in this poem is a belief that all glory and pride in physical magnificence will pall before death, certainly a theme long in the mind of man but a strange one to find in this age of sensuality. It does not, however, seem out of place in the poems of an Ulster poet; for the harshness and anger of his divided land cannot absent themselves from anything that grows out of the culture.

Of course, much here resembles life and attitudes in any agrarian community, but not in the experience of most westerners — certainly not if they live in the United States. Heaney's people have been merged with the land and its demands. Probably consciously recalling the struggle of the animals, Heaney describes peasants digging potatoes:

> Centuries
> Of fear and homage to the famine god
> Toughen the muscles behind their humbled knees,
> Make a seasonal altar of the sod.[32]

Such people have an integral part in the idea of Ireland that has existed since the beginning of literature. The "humble peasant" became important to modern Irish literature because of the interests in folklore of the writers of the Irish Renaissance. And this attitude towards the peasant cloyed as these people began to leave rural Ireland for life in the cities. In the case of writers of this stock, humility had scant value in their personalities. With the rise of a realistic literature in the thirties, more attention was paid to the actual life of peasants and others among the poor. Heaney, with real force, continues that concern and does so without letting his people lapse into sociological studies or general "peasant types." They are Irish people whose lives deserve attention.

145

The specific forms, presented strongly, form the body of Heaney's poetry, as he said in "The Peninsula," a poem about having nothing to say:

And drive back home, still with nothing to say
Except that now you will uncode all landscapes
By this: things founded clean on their own shapes,
Water and ground in their extremity.[33]

In two poems from his first volume, he suggests a complexity and tenderness that may well become more than implicit in his poetry. In "Docker" Heaney describes a man who frightens even his family when coming home from a pub:

That fist would drop a hammer on a Catholic —
Oh yes, that kind of thing could start again;
The only Roman collar he tolerates
Smiles all round his sleek pint of porter.[34]

This poem presents the harshness of the North with particular reference to angry Protestants. And though he calls attention to this bigoted attitude and contrasts it with a sympathetic Catholic one, Seamus Heaney is in no way biased.

All of Heaney's poetry is not bound by harshness, not even all of the religious poems. And when gaiety and love come, they are often bright and dancing, though sometimes stumbling. In "St. Francis and the Birds" occurs a startling contrast to much of Heaney's verse:

When Francis preached love to the birds
They listened, fluttered, throttled up
Into the blue like a flock of words
Released for fun from his holy lips.
Then wheeled back, whirred about his head,
Pirouetted on brothers' capes,
Danced on the wing, for sheer joy played
And sang, like images took flight.
Which was the best poem Francis made,
His argument true, his tone light.[35]

The relief into joy of a reader finding this poem makes him want to say, also, that this is the best poem Heaney made. But that is not true. The emptiness of *fun* in line four mars the poem, which also ends unexpectedly and rests upon a great deal of assumed information.

One must, perhaps, at this stage in Heaney's career accept his pared down diction as indicative of the way he views the world. His adjectives do not proliferate, and he is usually restrained. Also, recognition of the border is implicit in Heaney's poetry, not in theme but in subject. The poems about the North present the struggle and harshness of life, and the words of love come hesitatingly. But once away, he finds more tender subjects, as in "Girls Bathing, Galway 1965," from *Door Into the Dark:*

As through the shallows in swimsuits
Bare-legged, smooth-shouldered and long-backed
They wade ashore with skips and shouts.
So Venus comes, matter-of-fact.[36]

In his first volume, departure also occasioned a joyful lyric. As he described leaving Ireland with his bride:

And launched right off the earth by force of fire
We hang, miraculous, above the water,
Dependent on the invisible air
To keep us airbourne and to bring us further.[37]

Though more generally Irish than exclusively Northern, the necessity of exile may also be seen as characteristic of these tender poems. The importance Heaney gives to them is evidenced by the number of them he included on the recording he did with John Montague. On this record, *The Northern Muse*, three of the ten which Heaney read were from the tender, making the record scarcely a numerically representative selection. However, in the light of Heaney's observation that "the marriage/sex poems" form the heart of his second book, his reason for selecting the poems he read appears as other than a simple quantitative one.[38]

Judging from his more recent poems, Seamus Heaney prophesied in *The Northern Muse* the strength that would come from his merging of the harsh and the tender. "Limbo" is illustra-

147

tive. Here, a fisherman netted a drowned illegitimate infant, and Heaney reconstructs the scene of the mother holding him in the water:

> Till the frozen knobs of her wrists
> Were dead as gravel,
> He was a minnow with hooks
> Tearing her open.[39]

This poem illustrates the most recent stage in Seamus Heaney's growth into himself as a poet. He has accepted the responsibility of his art; for as he said, "Living through the past couple of years in this province has awakened me to the fact that a writer must be conscious that he is a political creature, even though he may eschew political subject matter."[40] This poem continues in an imaginary description of the mother, making the sign of the cross, as she consigns her child to limbo, that helpless place:

> But even Christ's palms, unhealed,
> Smart and cannot fish there.[41]

No mention of a political struggle or issue is made. However, the poem clearly identifies a Roman Catholic consciousness and in politically volatile Ulster could easily become a battle cry.

*Derek Mahon*     The poetry of Derek Mahon makes few references, direct or oblique, to the peculiarity of the Northern mind. Yet this young poet, like his elders, is conscious of his culture and its demands. In an article about Kavanagh he said, "As a Northerner I have a vested interest in the late Louis MacNeice, but if we take Dr. Conor Cruise O'Brien's definition of an Irish poet ('One who is involved in the Irish situation, and usually mauled by it') I am convinced that Patrick Kavanagh was the finest Irish poet since Yeats."[42] Why Cruise O'Brien's pub-wit definition should become a public dictum needs explanation and qualification. But Kavanagh had a quality dear to the younger poets in Ireland today, especially those having alliances with English publishing houses. Kavanagh's sardonic crust gave him a distance from his subject that all the Northern poets (including MacNeice) lack.

People with such a check on sentiment the contemporary critical mind generally regards with favor, especially if the two happen to be Irish and dead. Perhaps these are reasons for Mahon's praise. Much more convincing, however, is his description of MacNeice:

> The ironical, loving crush of roses against snow,
> Each fragile, solving ambiguity. So
> From the pneumonia of the ditch, from the ague
> Of the blind poet and the bombed-out town you bring
> The all-clear to the empty holes of spring,
> Rinsing the choked mud, keeping the colours new.[43]

As important as shared country of birth, implied in Mahon's mention of MacNeice, is their shared experience. Though at different points in their personal chronology, both entered the last part of the twentieth century through World War II. Memories and stories of the War, as Mahon said, give him an understanding of the dweller in London or Coventry not open to a Southern poet.[44] And this same experience must limit his understanding of life in the South, though he has chosen to center his literary life at the present in Dublin. War, shipyard, industry have produced a living and often disturbing culture in the North.

Reminiscent of John Montague's attitude in "The Siege of Mullingar" is Mahon's saying he would rather live in a real culture of flashing colored lights and jukeboxes than in the artificial one created by the writers of the Celtic Renaissance.[45] In "My Wicked Uncle" Mahon approvingly compares his roguish uncle with the next generation:

> His teenage kids are growing horns and claws —
> More wicked already than ever my uncle was.[46]

In "First Principles" Mahon tells how a poem he wants to write differs from the usual ones about women and then categorizes his intended poem. In it the refusal to avoid raw, though real, emotions fits well with the idea (or mask) of the Northern Irish poet which I have been developing:

> No, it will so derange
> The poor bitches, that they
> Will come round on their knees

> At all hours of the day,
> Crippled with visceral rage
> And croaking please, please.[47]

Love and tenderness, needed and sought after, are not nourished by the culture of Northern Ireland. Even the poets must struggle like vines in poor ground. A poem about Robert Flaherty illustrates this situation. Here Mahon, in a form he often uses, assumes the personality of his subject and speaks as Flaherty:

> The relief to be out of the sun —
> To have travelled north once more
> To my islands of dark ore,
> Where winter is so long
> Only a little light
> Gets through, and that perfect.[48]

The desire for and the awareness of joy are very real here, again typifying the Northern poet who must often leave his community yet seems either unable or unwilling to forget his origin and its responsibilities.

Mahon concerns his poetry with the important themes of his time and place in general, late twentieth-century Europe. The psychological problems of people trying for at least verbal communication belong to him as does an awareness that people in his specific place and time need his attention. This realization gnaws through to the reader in the poem, "In Belfast":

> One part of my mind must learn to know its place —
> The things that happen in the kitchen-houses
> And echoing back-streets of this desperate city
> Should engage more than my casual interest,
> Exact more interest than my casual pity.[49]

That he knows so much of himself and is a poet of growing power in the North explains the attention he has received from *The Honest Ulsterman*, which has not only published him but quite approvingly reviewed *Night Crossing*, a term generally meaning passage to England, where Mahon has so many literary ties. Edna Longley, a friend of his, has aptly described his talent: "Although his technique has been assisted by various influences (Baudelaire,

Graves, MacNeice, Dylan Thomas) Mahon's roots are unwillingly in Ulster. . . ."[50] But Mahon, though he may recognize these roots, has aspiration to grow other ones, as he suggests in "Exit Molloy," the last section of "Four Walks in the Country near Saint Brieuc":

> Now at the end I smell the smells of spring
> Where in a dark ditch I lie wintering —
> And the little town only a mile away,
> Happy and fatuous in the light of day.
> A bell tolls gently. I should start to cry
> But my eyes are closed and my face dry.
> I am not important and I have to die.
> Strictly speaking, I am already dead,
> But still I can hear the birds sing on over my head.[51]

Edna Longley comments that Mahon's "heroes are usually both isolated and down and out — Van Gogh, De Quincey, Molloy." True. And as she has also said, he "relates the (literal) microcosm to the macrocosm with an Elizabethan density. . . ."[52] Beckett rather than any sonneteer seems a more likely and immediate reference, for he presents his world as ineluctable and nonontological: a fact. Mahon, though, remains too committed to man trying for human intercourse to adopt the complete factualism and internationalism of Beckett.

Mahon's most recent enterprise enforces the perplexity of forces working on him: the founding with several friends of a new journal, *Atlantis*. The title itself suggests the recovery of a lost land all assume to have been preferable to what remained above the waters. Its purpose as described in the editorial of the first issue is a familiar one to readers of Irish literary periodicals:

> The magazine will be published in Dublin, but not exclusively for Dublin. The range of contributors will be wide. Part of our aim is to see Ireland in an international perspective, to lift its drowsy eyelid and disturb it into a sense of relationship and awareness.[53]

It is not to be simply a literary magazine since it will attempt to criticize the national spirit. With such a statement, the editors need not say they will in part be political, but they do. Indeed, as

Seamus Heaney observed, one does not have to be political in subject to have political relevance.

Undoubtedly, both the border and the civil rights struggle in the North will be important in the periodical — as well as for Mahon, who mentioned they would become so in his own poetry.[54] However, the tone of the comments in *Atlantis* surprises, though the presence of an article by Conor Cruise O'Brien, newly elected Labor Party member of the Irish Parliament, is quite suggestive, as is a reference to James Connolly in the editorial.[55]

In the second issue of *Atlantis*, Seamus Heaney in a review of commentaries on Northern Ireland, entitled "Mugwumps and Reptiles," took a strongly socialist approach to the animosities aroused to violence in the North:

> Ireland must recognize the nature of her problem. It is social, economic and moral. It is not religious or racial or nationalist. Obviously such a recognition would mean a movement to the left by the general mass of the people.[56]

He is aware that this was Marx's view of Irish discontent and cites Engels. He does not, however, mention that during his stay in Ireland, Engels repeatedly asked Marx to relieve him of his mission there because the problem was nationalism not economics.[57] Perhaps *Atlantis* from the South will add further arguments to those from its brother in the North, *The Honest Ulsterman*. Issues three and four of *Atlantis* have not, however, contained revolutionary poems or essays. Instead they have been thoughtful considerations of the self (especially the modern Irish). That honesty is the method and program of both heartens, but one wonders how long ingrained rancor will need before common sense will deprive Ireland of its burden/incentive: narrow hostility that has fostered as many literary revolutions as it has political rebellions.

### CHAPTER VIII

# The New Writers' Press

Michael Smith, editor of the New Writers' Press, publishes in a variety of formats what, at first glance, seems to be a very wide range of Irish poetry. Some volumes are bound, some are in paper covers, a few appear in both, and some appear in neither. The latter are called "versheets," a page folded in quarters, printed on three sides, and glued to a paper cover. Also, he publishes *The Lace Curtain*, a periodical, now in its fourth issue. The poets range from the living and dead who are best known for their writings in the 1930's to those just barely in their 20's. In spite of this seeming variety and the somewhat misleading name of the press, a marked characteristic identifies almost all of the poets as belonging to the same family: the intellectual verse which Pound and Eliot passed on to Beckett. The New Writers' Press is quite selective and makes clear in polemics, essays, poems, and information on the covers of volumes that the selection has been made to present a coherent body of poetry written in Ireland by and for a cultural elite.

*Thomas MacGreevy*

Thomas MacGreevy's *Collected Poems* reprints the 1934 issue of his *Poems* with the addition of five previously uncollected pieces. The "Afterword" by Thomas Dillon Redshaw and the introduction by Samuel Beckett, reprint of a 1934 review, make clear that MacGreevy's place is among the modernist verse of Eliot. "Manifesto," printed at the back of the volume is signed by Hans Arp, Samuel Beckett, Carl Einstein, Eugene Jolas, Thomas MacGreevy, and others: "We reject the postulate that the

creative personality is a mere factor in the pragmatic conception
of progress, and that its function is the delineation of a vitalistic
world."[1] Poetry, then, is the poet's act of awareness, his recognition of the mind's reality, most often expressed through surrealis-
tically structured images which become metaphors:

> White manes tossed like spray.
> Bluish snakes slid
> Into the dissolution of a smile.[2]

The rhetorician's play with words which simultaneously suggests a
spiritual ontology (part of Eliot's technique) appears often in
MacGreevy's poetry:

> The sun burns out,
> The world withers
> And time grows afraid of the triumph of time.[3]

This, too, delineates the heritage of MacGreevy, which he
acknowledges in his notes to the poems.[4]

Even in poems distinctly Irish, he wrote to establish in Ireland a kinship with the new writing of his time rather than to
invigorate *whatever* native traditions could be found. "*Cron Trath
Na nDeithe*," written Easter Saturday, 1923, avoids both the
traumatic romanticism of nineteenth-century patriotic verse and
the realism of the street found in some contemporary Ulster
poetry. Instead in clever, poised wordplay, he castigates those
who let revolution and culture fail:

> They are gone, they are gone
> Gandon and Smyth
> We have no Smygandons to-day
> Our Smyths bloom discreetly in narcissus beds
> In matrimonial suburbs
> Our Gandons turn mariner
> And, quarrelling, sail oceans.[5]

The note to the poem defines the title as "an Irish equivalent for
the German word *Gotterdammerung*" and identifies the two men
named: Edward Smyth was a sculptor and James Grandon an
architect. Much of the beauty of eighteenth-century Dublin

which remains was created by them. Though excusing himself from the intention of lauding Georgian Dublin, he clearly prized the cultural achievement of the time.[6] And he equally censured the rising middle-class power.

He was unwilling to abandon place for the mental reality of Eliot's wasteland or to accept Yeats's metaphoric artifice of Ireland as reality. He remains, as Beckett observed, between the two and "an existentialist in verse."[7]

*Brian*
*Coffey*

As the New Writers' Press did with Mac-Greevy so with Brian Coffey. Poems that have been unavailable in a single volume now are. As well as *Selected Poems*, some were also printed in a versheet. The larger volume covers the years 1931-1971 and illustrates Coffey's constant concern with modern European verse and, significantly, with his home. That home has not always been, and is not now, in Ireland.

Coffey's two concerns do not always appear in a single poem, understandably, since the merger is a curious one. "Davy Byrne's Of A Saturday Night" has some of the flavor of that Dublin pub, but the images are not left in native structures:

> But to continue meditating on life:
> There are a number of ways of irritating people.
> Observe the big black woman with a knife
> Chasing Poe's raven up that steeple.[8]

As is customary with writers coming from modernism, images are ordered in structures determined by an intellectual, or spiritual, reality revealed through metaphor:

> At last the pure rock
> faced the acid weather
> through year by thousand year
> while tempered beak
> on glass rock
> no purchase found.[9]

155

As Beckett explained in his essay, "Recent Irish Poetry," reprinted in *The Lace Curtain*, Coffey and Devlin distinguish themselves from Yeats and his followers by being aware of themselves, by admitting in poems "The existence of the author."[10] The personages of legend who have become personae have no place in this poetry, but unlike many who resisted the influence of Yeats, the Irish modernists did not also reject metaphoric structures.

As strong an influence on Coffey as his chosen literary tradition is his conception of himself as Irish. In "Missouri Sequence," poems of goodbye to America, he wrote clear, unmetaphoric images: as he described his children's way of life:

> They know nothing of Ireland,
> they grow American.
> They have chased snakes through the couch-grass
> in summer, caught butterflies and beetles
> we did not know existed,
> fished for catfish,
> slept on an open porch. . . .[11]

Their home is physical, but not his: "Return home takes on while I dream it/ the fictive form of heaven on earth. . . ."[12] What his children know in America, Irish poets of a later generation would know in Ireland. This sequence of poems, written in 1962, often gently presents the fact, unadorned while moving into metaphor:

> I would choose, I suppose, yet would be chosen
> in some equation between God's will and mine,
> rejecting prudence to make of conflict
> a monument to celtic self-importance.[13]

The image here is God, and the metaphor "celtic," the first a fact for Coffey and the latter a conception, inescapable but nevertheless a conception which gave birth to his existence.

*Anthony Cronin*    After the thirties necessarily came the forties, the wane of the Renaissance under the attack of the internationalists, with Cronin giving intellectual weight and direction to Patrick Kavanagh's scattered attacks and insults. Cronin's *Collected Poems* traces the splintering of his force against the more professional poets who matured after he fought the battles and lost the war. Ireland was not ready to accept a professional man of letters of a mold other than Yeats's, and Cronin was not willing to make literature a means to university position or to a governmental position. At least, he would have us so believe; and he may be right.

The plays on words, the acts of intellect that characterized the poets before him became Cronin's guidelines. But never in his poetry was he able to be so abstract, so rhetorical, as to remove completely his immediate sensing of experience. He seldom described the experience itself, and at his best wrote of reactions many have shared. "Surprises" begins as a facile, sardonic lyric:

> Since we are told it we believe it's true,
> Or does as it's intended. Birds eat worms,
> The water flows downhill and aunts depart.

But the last stanza strikes a note of bitterness to become predominant when Cronin no longer has all of his future before him:

> Nothing is order now and no forecast
> Can be depended on since what's declared
> To be may not be so, and each face wears
> A false expression. Yet the very last
> Surprise of all finds us unprepared:
> Although we say I love you no one cares.[14]

Man, not Irishman, is Cronin's constant reference, occurring as it does in "A Revenant" and being tied to a precedent in "For the Damned Part":

> This is the way the world goes,
> The dead twig in the ground,
> The bottle by the lakeside
> While winter gathers round.[15]

The first line clearly recalls Eliot's "The Hollow Men," and one could at this time easily drop Cronin into the existential slot.[16]

However, his problem is Irish, and he regards it as such. Neither he nor any of the contemporary Irish poets have been able to convince themselves that life can be as abstract, as mythological, as religious as Eliot tried to present it in all phases of his writing. Their land, as Coffey said, is "fictive." Separated from it, they must reconstruct it as Joyce did or write of the separation as Cronin did:

> And now having chosen, with strangers,
> Half glad of his choice,
> He smiles with his father's hesitant smile
> And speaks with his voice.[17]

Perhaps the cynicism, the intellectual acts but mask his inability to abstract himself completely from the weight of his cultural identity. His own explanation is the time in which he lived:

> I could disown them like a thirties poet
> And yet I set inexplicables down,
> And scattered images of London when
> With a true love I could most truly know it.[18]

These "inexplicables" reoccur frequently. They are called images, images without metaphoric structure, and they are his "grave reality":

> A dray rolls down South King Street,
> The setts are warm outside,
> A faint sea breeze in Stephen's Green
> Ruffles the typists' pride.[19]

But Ireland after the revolution is no more welcoming to him than it would have been before, and like his predecessors in the thirties, he scorns the opportunists. Or are they but the ones who found a place? In "Lunchtime Table, Davy Byrne's" this question cannot be avoided:

> Behold inheritors.
> For them the grey geese spread
> Etcetera and Paudeen in damp grass
> Stared up at four-cloaked prophets on a hill

Promising nation states, proprietors,
Communes and comfort, final freedom from
The caubeen and the caub, the cold potato so
That the wise Gaelic could flow free again
And ecumenical Dominicans absolve
And Beckett follow Joyce to give a cachet
To jobs concerned with handouts, trade and art.[20]

Here Cronin rejects the early arrogant hope, surety even, and approaches (by allusion) Yeats's assessment of his countrymen as trivial-minded, opportunistic. But for whatever reason, hope or talent, Cronin does not have Yeats's structure to direct his life even in the midst of dissolution and the resulting despair.

Many of the later poems lack the exactness of diction, do not show the intellectual deftness of earlier ones, but do show the dangers of his tutelage under Patrick Kavanagh. "The Irish Great Poetry Boom, 1970s" is "The Paddiad" in contemporary dress with the envy and the anger re-directed:

Yeats, Yeats, Yeats, Yeats,
Clarke, Clarke, Clarke, Clarke,
Kavanagh, Kavanagh, Kavanagh, . . .
'These we know are the true greats.'
Yeats, Yeats, Yeats, Yeats.
Fart, fart, fart, fart.[21]

Even the apology that "poor P.K." was not responsible and would be offended by the accolades (which should endear this study to him) do not decrease the anger which scatters out to include "Kinsella, Kinsella, Kinsella, Kinsella" and "the other fellow" whoever he may be.[22] Many of the last poems repeat the statement. "To Some We Know Of" says he could have chosen a way with more conventional rewards.[23] "On A Change In Literary Fashion" is from the Irish of Eochaidh O hEoghusa, a seventeenth-century poet, but suits well Cronin's tone in these poems. He blames his lack of recognition among the givers of reward on a "new fashion" that does not respect mastery of skills

159

and understands only "loose and artless" writing which he will provide for those who pay since the old ways are gone anyway.

The intent of The New Writers' Press is to attack the existing powers in contemporary poetry by reloading old guns and pointing them in new directions while at the same time establishing a tradition in modern Irish verse counter to that which binds together such disparate poets as Kinsella, Montague, and Murphy. Taking part of the technique of poets in the thirties as the most important, the New Writers' Press has asserted the existence of a strong and constant belief in abstract thought and poetry for the elite within the development of contemporary Irish poetry.

**James Liddy**

Liddy's versheet, *Homage to Patrick Kavanagh*, is only partially accurate in title. The opening sentence sets a tone that whatever homage is paid never succeeds in dominating: "We have again the time of bosses." The tone is, unmistakably, that of Kavanagh in *Envoy*. Only the object (target) has changed because Yeats no longer troubles the poets, with the possible exception of Clarke, who does not have intercourse with Liddy and his group. Yeats, in fact, is only briefly mentioned. He was a "boss" and so ruled, creating a time when poetry was a product, not something "on its own." And the mention occurred only as a contrast to Kavanagh, who gave and did not sell. What he gave was love. To whom is not mentioned.

The real object of this essay is anyone among the contemporary poets who can be termed a "boss," i.e., someone who makes a living by putting poetry into the marketplace. Only one is mentioned: "The bosses of today, with the partial exception of Mr. Kinsella, the ablest writer among them, prefer non-physical rhythms."[24] The term "non-physical rhythms" is one best left for the Dublin literati to play with, but essentially it means literature proceeding from literature rather than from life. Who else among the contemporary poets may be called a boss is left to speculation. But Montague and Murphy have been successful, have both made money in American universities (as have Liddy and Kinsella), and have both put poetry in the theatre. Dublin, one must remember, does not forgive success, but does not consider failure to be desirable.

Liddy's actual concern with Kavanagh is anecdotal and evaluative: "Paddy embodied love," an assertion unsupported by the anecdotes.[25] What is proven, however, is that James Liddy belonged to the inner circle, knew the man, his opinions, who was in and who out. Some very good writers seemed to have survived and prospered without such intimacy: "Once in McDaid's unaccustomed faces appeared: Thomas Kinsella, Richard Murphy, George MacBeth."[26] What separates these three from Kavanagh and what links Liddy and Kavanagh is not explained, but implication is made and has been made by several of the writers already discussed in this chapter. Poetry is for an elite, an end in itself, an end that cannot be achieved in popular performance.

*Michael*
*Hartnett*

Michael Hartnett was also an editor of *Arena*, which in part explains why the New Writers' Press published two of his books. Also, the publication of *Tao* (first issued by *Arena*) and *Selected Poems* makes available poems by a good younger poet. His work fits well into the structure so far described in being internationalist and by paying deference to elitist verse. *Tao* is based on sixth-century Chinese poetry and recalls the Eastern based poetry so much in vogue during the sixties, in no way making the poems insincere. But the poems do recall the concern of *Arena* with the American anti-war movement: "No lord, I will not give battle:/ let the people come and burn my house."[27] Missing now in these and the rest of Hartnett's poems is concern with violence and civil disorder in Ireland.

Instead, he continues to write of man, not Irishman. His practice resembles Eliot's theory of criticism: what writers have in common and not what distinguishes one from another is of primary concern.[28] Perhaps for this reason no names are used in the series called "Notes on my Contemporaries 1969." Identifiable

161

are Kavanagh in "The Poet Down" and Desmond O'Grady in "The Poet As Exile," which in the last two lines echoes O'Grady's tentative dirge for art in our time: "By the fountains of Rome/ we sat down and wept."[29]

Most of his poems commend the small gestures and struggles that typify contemporary, perhaps all, life. And humanity here finds moments of care to be treasured. "Her Diadem . . ." tells of his meeting with a woman he had loved who had achieved recognition for her poetry after they parted: "she saw me and she/ shook my hand."[30] In "I Have Managed" he tells of coping with life:

the heart survives
and learns to live
with second-rate pictures
and second-rate hysteria.[31]

Thoreau's "quiet desperation" comes to mind, indicating both the present viability of the phrase and the truth of Hartnett's poem.

Most of the poems are familiar in style: lack of conversational diction, willingness to play with rhyme, some venturing into modernist metaphor. But one poem departs from the expected, "Crossing the Iron Bridge":

"There will be the glow of God in your veins, your souls will be at one with Heaven: if you were to die today, angels would open the Gates of Paradise, and with great rejoicing bear you in . . ."

Back to the human-hampered light,
my arms in white rosettes,
I walked: my faith was dead.
Instead of glory on my tongue
there was the taste of bread.[32]

Other poems also written in 1966 have a similar concern with childhood and the pangs of growing up in rural Ireland, though unspecified in the poem.

Leland Bardwell's *The Mad Cyclist* contains more "serious" poetry in theme and technique than seemed representative of her work
before it was collected. The carelessly bold
stroke that characterized her poetry before, and delighted her
readers, is scarcely in evidence. Much of the poetry in this volume
is polysyllabic, intellectual, and foreign. For instance, "The Mad
Cyclist":

Such arrogance must be prevented
such unnatural practices stopped
or have her certificated
for putative felo-de-se
but she with her revs circumvented
their aims and cried 'ou est mon velo'
like Cocteau to Diaghialev
when the latter said 'J'suis étoné.'

Kafka and F. Scott Fitzgerald are subjects. And even Yeats and
Lady Gregory are treated with a touch of, if not touching, nostalgia.[33]

The concern with contemporary life, however, does occur in
these poems. Abortion and the corruption of a tinsel world are
subjects.[34] And "Flowers For Three Dead Men" comes from the
time of *Arena*:

I. was a low-sized lad from Belfast
Who made me along the quays
On a night and a day against
Arm or winch or spar
Or something cold like a midnight steel
Where a seagull dips
And waters discreetly lap
As the Liffey's lazy mouth
Yawns into the sea.
We kipped in a B. & B.
The following night. . . .[35]

Though this volume shows the variety of themes Leland Bardwell works with, the exclusion of more poems such as this is regrettable, though predictable. Poetry, here, is a "serious" matter.

*Trevor Joyce*

Trevor Joyce, who edits the versheets, has published three books of poems with the New Writers' Press. The information inside the front cover of *Pentahedron*, the most recent, supports the main contention of this chapter: "His two previous collections, *Sole Glum Trek* and *Watches*, solidly established him as one of the best Irish poets to have emerged since the Thirties." The touchstone appears again. And Trevor Joyce's new volume places him solidly in the modernist tradition.

Basic to Joyce's technique is the image occurring within a metaphoric structure designed to link what had never before been linked, to paraphrase Johnson's definition of the metaphysical conceit.[36] As, for instance, "Plague": "Why do you leave the tall granite arch of my mind's night,/ you with the parrot eyes?"[37] Giving force and direction to the metaphor, in this and others, is modernist disgust with physicality:

Acts are expectorated,
and when the spittle hardens
into facts, our lives
are emerald threads of mucous.[38]

Neither the images nor the words are unexpected in this poem, but instead seem fitting and even traditional.

Unlike so many of the poets discussed in this book, Joyce and most of the others with the New Writers' Press do not work with colloquial diction. As in the poem above, the words are proper, polysyllabic, and not of the street. The comment itself may have a contemporary reference, if a temporal one is called for, but the language usually remains within the bindings of a dictionary. Words not previously (i.e., in the nineteenth century) used in poetry do occur, as in *"The Roads, People, The River (Soured With Industrial Excrement) & Town:"*. Even the title of this poem illustrates the modernist way with words as the parenthetical comment refers to a contemporary problem with words not used in poems during the last century. The poem, however, does not further any immediate shock; but remains within the level of usage intelligent and educated people have traditionally found comfortable:

> like golden ants upon their backs their own apprehension,
> flock into his skull and make their nest, and breed,
> what more reason for a bird's rapture?[39]

Though the poem is about a derelict (society?), the language ironically removes itself from its subject's life, thus limiting the audience to readers who like intellectual games, word play.

*Augustus Young* Augustus Young has published two books with The New Writers' Press. *Survival*, the first: "introduced Irish readers to the rigorously impassioned intelligence that characterizes the poems and experiments in *On Loaning Hill*," the second book.[40] The language remains within the modernist tradition:

> Lonely for you, night finds me
> a moon perhaps, an aspirin
> to burn me white.[41]

He does not depart from this expected range of language or metaphoric technique, nor should he since both please him and are effective.

Young does have political concerns, again within the expected range. Ireland does not arouse his concern as much as "My Lai" and America:

> The skies dirty over, poison
> observes a multi-layer.
> And Martin Luther King's brother
> fixed to the tiles of his private
> swimming pool (Just like young Jones).[42]

This poem, called "From A Newspaper," mentions the Pope and birth control in Ireland but clearly faces west, repeating the nearly desperate internationalists' attempt to be involved in the big world.[43] Neglected is Ireland's rising violence and declining economy.

*John*
*Jordan*

John Jordan, who knows the course of contemporary Irish literature so thoroughly, illustrates in *Patrician Stations* a probable cause for the brevity and infrequency of his publications. The second poem in the first section, "A Guest of the Dean's," recalls a stay in St. Patrick's Hospital for the cure:

> The Eye of Heaven blazes on the strollers
> In the Gardens of *Welldorm*: did the bats
> Come in the middle of the night? The cats tie themselves
> To your body? The scimitars castrate you?
> The *Artane* Band parades among the roses.
> The Legion of Gardenal inspects the dahlias.
> (Great Dean, your people, yours and mine, call them day-
> lias)[44]

The identification made between two tormented minds, between two self-besieged poets, seems fitting.

The immediacy of Jordan's poems removes them from the established pattern of The New Writers' Press, and the act of intellect involved in the poems is a modernist one without the usual metaphoric structure. The second poem in "The Feast of St. Justin" desanctifies divinities: "But Mary forgiving Jesus for his brusquerie,/ This, my children, is of the minutae of daily experience."[45] This recognition, celebration even, of flawed humanity characterizes the poetry of John Jordan and parallels it, curiously, with that of Paul Murray, a member of the Dominican order.

*Paul*
*Murray*

In *Ritual Poems*, he presents the priest as flawed humanity. "Death Of A Priest" is illustrative:

> A black breviary propped between his
> Chest and chin, a cold

Hand closing his eyes, touching
Without chrism his wrinkled forehead;
Only then could he believe
She was neither fantasy of daydream
Nor temptation: Death.[46]

All the poems are quiet and restrained, but do not remove themselves from the physical humanity of man. Intellect does not become an end, the definition of man.

*Desmond* *O'Grady*          Though largely concerned with the tradition of the thirties that continues into the present, the New Writers' Press has obviously published poets not working within the pure form. Desmond O'Grady in *Hellas* is such a poet. This series of poems presents his anger and sorrow with the military government in Greece. He was there during the time of the takeover and writes of friends who were victimized, of the traditions of love and friendship ignored by the junta, and of the ancient misery of his own country. Recalling a night in Greece when a friend threatened by arrest appeared, he recalled walking home and the "old song came into my head/ from my own country":

I am Ireland
I am older than the Hag of Baer Island
Great my pride
It was I bore brave Cuchulainn
Great my shame
My own family sold their mother
I am Ireland
I am lonelier than the Hag of Baer Island.[47]

As always, the poetry of O'Grady is sure, learned, and immediate whether the subject is ancient Greece and Ireland or modern man. Though he does not fit within anyone else's structures, his kinship with Ezra Pound should endear him to The New Writers' Press.

167

Working selectively with the poetry of contemporary Ireland, The New Writers' Press has established a tradition. Let us hope that a desire to combat and destroy poets of other modes will not in turn destroy the attackers, as so often has happened with movements in contemporary Ireland.

### CHAPTER IX

# Poetry of Outsiders

Though the poets in Ireland since World War II have frequently formed literary and political alliances, no prolific writer has maintained a closeness with a particular group. Whether the poet be one who soon matured and faded or one who grew gradually into power, no group could nourish his talent. The reason for this may well be the loss of England as a central theme. Without "the oppression of the dirty Saxon foe" to serve as a target for all of the writers' anger and disappointment with life in Ireland, they turned upon themselves with more fervor than usual — even in Ireland.

Deprived of the "spiritual nation," Irish writers found the actual Ireland too troubled and complex for their poetry. In the South, the failure of the 1916 Rebellion to effect a prosperous and free nation could not become a central theme, nor could the continuing insanity of the North. To accept these communities, in their sickness, would have held the poet to the past as surely as would copying the style of Yeats or Joyce, who looked at their nation torn by hatred and turned to a world of their own fabrication. But the new poets, unlike their predecessors, would not have a thing outside themselves and their culture to attack.

Also the idealized human being of nineteenth and early twentieth-century Irish literature could no longer interest writers who needed to make their own peace with troubled humanity. So their personae developed with all the flaws and intricacies that make people humanly interesting, though seldom magnificent. Even the poverty is different: a garret seems much more romantic than a bed-sitting room. Recent poets have not cut themselves off from all their past, national and personal. To use words and forms of writing that have been handled by generations of poets forces one into an acceptance, though perhaps a qualified one, of the past. The past is tied to the present in Ireland as strongly as it ever was; however the new writers insist upon the right to see it for themselves and not through the eyes of their parents and predecessors. Believing that all men share experiences of love, hate, hunger, fear, to name but a few, these poets cannot accept a view of Ireland that would self-consciously stress a separation between people on a simplistic national basis. Nor can they reject the earlier because they too share one another's experiences. In all, no matter what the era, flaws occur and sometimes dominate the personality. The recognition of these flaws which can incline one to anger as often as to love forms the real basis of the contemporary mode of writing.

No longer does the poet believe that a personified Ireland, especially an old woman who walked like a queen, can express the reality of his life, the forms of his desire. Not having this externalization of the self, the poet turns within and presents an often unfiltered portrayal of the self. Even if he skirts the subject, his inability to be a personage in the old grand manner makes him vulnerable to attack. Result: poetry of pain and joy and a group of quite aggressive and defensive poets.

Poetry proceeding from large systematized thought has not yet appeared. And it is doubtful that a fervor of systematizing will occur. The movements since the time of Yeats and Joyce have lacked the strict form and ontological values of the past. Instead, changes have come without benefit of the artist-priest who introduces the young into the mysteries of art and Irishry. No one figure attracts all to him because of his indisputably greater talent and genius. And no one functions as the communicator of a permanent and sacred knowledge. All centers have disappeared. Ireland itself remains a central concern to the poets but not in the old ontological way.

Recognition of man's imperfection has not led the writers to accept or approve of the government or general culture, both of which seem to have their characters determined by man's weaknesses more often than by his strengths. As did their predecessors, the contemporary poets rail at the hypocrisy, opportunism, cruelty, repressiveness of the established order. Belief that man can, or should, live with knowledge of his own temporary and insubstantial self has become a new, created culture. The people who live in such a culture would have to be able to suspend faith in future vindication and accept as inescapable that no one achieves an existence totally directed by principle. Of course, an existence predicated by such bases is impossible for most people and disastrous for many others. Patrick Kavanagh, for instance, developed a purposeless and indiscriminately destructive life, but one which reflects this concept.

The general ethical movement of contemporary Irish poetry, however, is not to inculcate amorality. The poetry, in general, purposefully extends the limits of liberal thought in the twentieth century. Traditionally, such thought has encouraged man to regard his fellows, and the environment, without bias or prejudice. The important addition of the poets in contemporary Ireland, as well as elsewhere, is the destruction of the subject-object relationship, the me-thou understanding of society. In the resulting concept of self, everyone must regard himself as warped by forces he can neither understand nor control. Obviously, the recognition that everyone is human did not just occur. But these poets illustrate very well the development of liberal-radical thought in the last half of this century. Much of the thought and action during this time has occurred as a direct result of an acceptance of man's flawed and irrational nature.

Neither the poets nor the poetry has been limited to describing existence without attempting to perceive real and universal patterns of behavior. The dangers are the same as always: the knowledge forms patterns, and the patterns form binding schemes which prescribe actions and identities. The result can easily be repetitive art and inert life. At the present time, the writers are active, though repeated themes (such as Kinsella's series of ordeals) and repeated forms (such as the long poems of Montague and Murphy) occur. Only in a culture demanding individuality would such repetition seem dangerous or compromising. The writers themselves certainly recognize the similarities among them, though frequently reject one another stylistically.

The long poems, in particular, illustrate a growing confidence among the poets and an increased understanding of their reference to the culture which has produced them. The long poem always presents serious problems for the writer, but Ginsberg's answer to my question, "How do you write a long poem?" may be everyone's. He said that a writer must extend himself, write everything he knows about the subject; and when he gets through, he has a long poem.[1] "Extend himself" deserves emphasis. More so than in other English-speaking countries, the past verges on the present in Ireland. One must in any long, complex understanding of himself extend into the past. But few of the poets writing today have wanted to preserve that past in a museum. Mahon and Montague, for instance, welcome the entrance of vital, though often crude, forces to invigorate the culture. Past, present, future form a continuum that can only be kept alive by the introduction of the new and can only be kept constant by the preservation of the past. The past is known, the present suggested, the future unknown. The excitement of a poetry in which the possibility of humanity forms the stimuli is great.

Now that the immediate literary and political past in Ireland is growing less threatening, as it grows more distant, poets can approach the totality of their society with more ease and confidence. The general society, however, continues to develop a banality and materialism that have become significant characteristics of the growing mass culture. In Ireland the manners of the past still encourage a degree of casualness and generosity not as frequently found in England or America.

Except for the importance of the new, crude vigor and the interest in the past, Samuel Beckett might have become a major example and influence in contemporary Irish poetry. His concern with the separate individual, the outsider, in novels is an important parallel to the poetry examined in this book. The loneliness of Beckett resembles that in Ireland today, but his is that of purposeless people awaiting death. The greater majority of the

Irish writers are waiting for a new awareness to unite the society or, at least, the writers. Beckett, as do Camus and Sartre, offers a systematic approach to existence; but he does so to reject the possible emergence of a vital ontology. He is a Descartian who has suspended fear of and faith in God, as in "Whoroscope":

A wind of evil flung my despir of ease
against the sharp spires of the one
lady:
nor once or twice but. . . .
(Kip of Christ hatch it!)
in one sun's drowning
(Jesuitasters please copy).
So on with the silk hose over the knitted, and
          the morbid leather —
what am I saying! the gentle canvas[2]

In this ironical treatment of Descartes' "visions and pilgrimage to Loretto" Beckett ridicules the philosopher with accusations of illogical reasoning, which are true. But now such a studied rejection, complete with notes, seems unwarranted. Granted, Descartes initiated much that European man has been pressured by since, but Beckett allows his comment to be controlled by the subject. He does not move into the present as he does so well in his novels, which laugh so humorlessly at man made into a pawn by the systems he invents.

Few of the contemporary Irish writers are capable of such abstract concerns, and they would be abstract to writers accepting the new or the old as capable of revitalization. Such bleakness and estrangement would seem artificial from anyone incapable of cultural isolation to the extent Beckett is. And the Irish poets today are becoming, sometimes by necessity, involved in the processes of their society. The possibility of an *engagé* art becomes ever greater. For all the debunking of the past that began as a theme in the forties and became an occasional comment as the seventies began, the Irish poets repeat attitudes similar to those of their predecessors. Though with a different understanding, the contemporaries believe in the value of the land itself and in the people. Civilization, for many, remains Irish culture. Tempered by a changing world and a new realization of man, they yet wait for the center to gather itself and inform all. That may well be the strongest similarity among writers today of whatever culture. But the Irish know so well from their recent history the beauty, force, and anguish created when all facets of a life respond to a single cue. They also know the difficulty of reconstructing belief and art when the center has gone. The Irish poets, though they may at times need a center of belief, will be long in accepting one. And poetry will be the work of outsiders who would be surprised to see the characteristics they all share.

# Notes

## Chapter I

1. THE COLLECTED POETRY OF W. H. AUDEN (New York, 1945), p. 50.
2. William Butler Yeats, THE AUTOBIOGRAPHY OF WILLIAM BUTLER (Garden City, 1958), p. 77.
3. THE COLLECTED POEMS OF W. B. YEATS (New York, 1959), p. 343.
4. John Ryan showed a film he made of this walk at the Irish Sugar Company Cinema in Dublin on 17 June 1969.
5. "The People of Belfast," HOLIDAY, XXV: 2 (February, 1964), 62-63.
6. Henri Bergson, CREATIVE EVOLUTION (New York, 1913), p. 337.

## Chapter II

1. Conversation with Anthony Cronin in Milwaukee, Wisconsin, on 4 May 1969.
2. "Culture and Chauvinism," ENVOY, II: 6 (May, 1950), 75.
3. COLLECTED POEMS OF PATRICK KAVANAGH (New York, 1964), p. 5.
4. *Ibid.*, p. 17.
5. *Ibid.*, p. 14
6. *Ibid.*, p. 32.
7. *Ibid.*, p. 35.
8. *Ibid.*, p. 41.
9. "Auden and the Creative Mind," ENVOY, V: 19 (June, 1951), 34.
10. COLLECTED POEMS, p. 97.
11. *Ibid.*, p. 120.
12. *Ibid.*, p. 117.
13. *Ibid.*, xiv.
14. *Ibid.*, p. 100.
15. *Ibid.*, p. 191.
16. *Ibid.*, p. 188.
17. "Introduction," IRISH SHORT STORIES (London, 1960), p. 9.

18. THE DOLMEN MISCELLANY OF IRISH WRITING, ed. John Montague (Dublin, 1962), pp. 80-81.
19. "The Young Writer," THE BELL, XVII: 6 (September, 1951), 13.
20. THE COLLECTED POEMS OF W. B. YEATS (New York, 1959), p. 185.
21. "Robert Graves and the Sovereign Muse," THE BELL, XVII: 11 (February, 1952), 48.
22. RESERVATIONS (Dublin, 1950), p. 37.
23. COLLECTED POEMS (New York, 1966), pp. 175-176.
24. RESERVATIONS, p. 17.
25. *Ibid.,* p. 32.
26. *Ibid.*, p.18.
27. *Ibid.*, p. 23.
28. "The Young Writer," THE BELL, XVII: 6 (September, 1951), 8.
29. *Ibid.*, p. 12.
30. Alf McLoughlin, Keeper of the Printed Book, The National Library of Ireland, so described the gentleman while we were talking in Dublin during Horse Show Week in the summer of 1966.
31. POEMS (London, 1957), p. 1.
32. NEW POETS OF IRELAND (Denver, 1963), p. 109.
33. SELECTED POETRY OF W. H. AUDEN (New York, 1970), pp. 17, 114-117.
34. "The Young Writer," p. 6.
35. Pearse Hutchinson said to me in a conversation in Dublin on 2 July 1969 that ENVOY was important to him not only because the editors were friends and could give immediate payment but also because the concentration on internationalism was then a strong new force in his own writing and in Ireland.
36. (Dublin, 1963), p. 10.
37. *Ibid.*, p. 12.
38. *Ibid.*, p. 19.
39. *Ibid.*, p. 32.
40. Conversation with Pearse Hutchinson.
41. *Ibid.*

42. EXPANSIONS (Dublin, 1969), p. 50.
43. *Ibid.*, p. 21.
44. *Ibid.*, p. 9.
45. *Ibid.*, pp. 29-30, 48.
46. *Ibid.*, p. 14.


### Chapter III

1. Norman Podhoretz, MAKING IT (New York, 1967), p. 113
2. ARENA, II (Autumn, 1963), 1.
3. *Ibid.*, p. 23.
4. (Dublin, 1968), p. 14.
5. *Ibid.*, p. 13.
6. *Ibid.*, I (Spring, 1963), 17.
7. *Ibid.*, II, 20-21.
8. *Ibid.*, III, 11.
9. ARIEL (London, 1967), pp. 18-19.
10. "The Barfly Ought to Sing," TRI-QUARTERLY, 7 (Fall, 1966), 90.
11. ARENA, III, 11.
12. *Ibid.*, II, 5-6.
13. *Ibid.*, I (Spring, 1963), 20.
14. *Ibid.*, IV, 42.
15. *Ibid.*, p. 1.
16. *Ibid.*, III (Summer, 1964), 5.
17. (Dublin, 1962), p. 9.
18. *Ibid.*, p. 7.
19. (Dublin, 1964), p. 21.
20. BLUE SMOKE, p. 25.
21. *Ibid.*, p. 27.
22. *Ibid.*, p. 20.
23. *Ibid.*, p. 13.
24. *Ibid.*, p. 11.
25. *Ibid.*, p. 10.
26. *Ibid.*, p. 35.
27. *Ibid.*, p. 14.
28. Letter from John Montague dated 15 February 1969 from Paris, France.
29. I (Summer, 1965), 2.

30. *Ibid.*, p. 8.
31. THE HOLY DOOR, I (Summer, 1965), 3.
32. *Ibid.*, II (Autumn, 1965), 20.

*Chapter IV*

1. IRISH WRITING, 1 (1946), 7.
2. "The Irish Mode," POETRY IRELAND, 3 (October, 1948), 12-15.
3. *Ibid.*, 3 (July, 1948), 17.
4. IRISH WRITING, 12 (September, 1950), 23.
5. "Reviews 1946," POETRY IRELAND, 1 (April, 1948), 25.
6. "The Gallivanting Poet," IRISH WRITING, 3 (November, 1947), 69-70.
7. *Ibid.*
8. "Notes from a Journal," IRISH WRITING, 35 (Summer, 1956), 106.
9. Letter from Ewart Milne dated 12 March 1971, Bedford, England.
10. LISTEN MANGAN (Dublin, 1941), p. 8.
11. *Ibid.*, p. 47.
12. *Ibid.*, p. 35.
13. Milne made this summary of his involvement in the Spanish Civil War when I visited him in Bedford, England, 14 July 1969.
14. DIAMOND CUT DIAMOND (London, 1950), p. 23.
15. Letter from Ewart Milne dated 6 February 1969, Bedford, England.
16. LISTEN MANGAN, p. 37.
17. Letter dated 6 February 1969.
18. (Dublin, 1953), leaf 62v.
19. THE COLLECTED POEMS OF W. B. YEATS (New York, 1959), pp. 309, 314-315.
20. *Jubilo* (London, 1944), p. 46.
21. THE IRISH DEMOCRAT (August, 1949).
22. Letter from Milne dated 12 September 1969, Bedford, England.
23. THE IRISH DEMOCRAT.
24. A GARLAND FOR THE GREEN (London, 1962), p. 92.

25. THE COLLECTED POEMS OF W. B. YEATS, p. 264.
26. DIAMOND CUT DIAMOND, p. 60.
27. Letter dated 1 April 1971.
28. DIAMOND CUT DIAMOND, p. 15.
29. *Ibid.*, p. 16.
30. (London, 1958), p. 72.
31. *Ibid.*, pp. 22, 33-34, 12, 14-16.
32. (London, 1967), title page.
33. ONCE MORE TO TOURNEY, pp. 7-8.
34. *Ibid.*, p. 96.
35. I received this somewhat uneasy reaction when I mentioned Milne while visiting with some poets in Dublin during August of 1969.
36. TIME STOPPED, p. 81.
37. *Ibid.*, p. 106.
38. Interview with Milne on 14 July 1969.
39. TIME STOPPED, p. 148.
40. A PORTRAIT OF THE ARTIST AS A YOUNG MAN (New York, 1965), p. 203.
41. DIAMOND CUT DIAMOND, p. 10.
42. POETRY IRELAND, 1 (Autumn, 1962), 16.
43. Letter from Milne dated 1 April 1971.
44. Interview with Milne 14 July 1969.
45. POETRY IRELAND, 5 (April, 1949), 8.
46. No. 8 (July, 1949), 43-4. No. 11 (July, 1950).
47. SELECTED POEMS (New York, 1963).
48. P. 53.
49. POETRY IRELAND, 14 (July, 1951), 23.
50. COLLECTED POEMS (Dublin, 1964), pp. 114-115.
51. *Ibid.*, p. 115.
52. *Ibid.*, p. 111.
53. ART AND THE CREATIVE UNCONSCIOUS (New York, 1959), pp. 60-61.
54. COLLECTED POEMS, p. 116.
55. *Ibid.*, p. 93.
56. *Ibid.*, p. 99.
57. *Ibid.*, p. 96.
58. *Ibid.*, p. 35.

59. *Ibid.*, p. 37.
60. *Ibid.*, pp. 42-43, 45.
61. *Ibid.*, p. 75.
62. *Ibid.*, pp. 70-72.
63. *Ibid.*, p. 18.
64. The edition of this poem with variants and worksheets edited by Brian Coffey (THE HEAVENLY FOREIGNER, Dublin, 1967) does not intrinsically change one's understanding of the poem. Each section of the poem is entitled with name of a city, indicating a sequential rather than essentially organic development.
65. COLLECTED POEMS, pp. 23-24.
66. *Ibid.*, pp. 29-30.
67. *Ibid.*, p. 31.
68. COSMOS AND HISTORY (New York, 1959), pp. 85-86.
69. COLLECTED POEMS, pp. 31-32.
70. *Ibid.*, p. 17.
71. IRISH WRITING, 8 (July, 1949), 57.
72. POETRY IRELAND, 3 (October, 1948), 7.
73. POETRY IRELAND, 7 and 8 (Spring, 1968), 107.
74. No. 4 (April, 1948), 25.
75. Interview with Liam Miller, Dublin, 27 June 1969.

*Chapter V*
1. (Dublin, 1951), p. 41.
2. *Ibid.*, pp. 14-16.
3. THE COLLECTED POEMS OF AUSTIN CLARKE (London, 1936), p. 229.
4. *Ibid.*, p. 267.
5. THE COLLECTED POEMS OF W. B. YEATS (New York, 1959), p. 240.
6. POETRY IN MODERN IRELAND (Cork, n.d.), pp. 53-54.
7. COLLECTED POEMS OF AUSTIN CLARKE, p. 50.
8. POETRY IN MODERN IRELAND, p. 42.
9. COLLECTED POEMS OF AUSTIN CLARKE, p. 312.
10. *Ibid.*, p. 313.
11. COLLECTED POEMS OF W. B. YEATS, p. 200.

12. COLLECTED POEMS OF AUSTIN CLARKE, p. 57.
13. A TRIBUTE TO AUSTIN CLARKE ON HIS SEVEN-TIETH BIRTHDAY (Dublin, 1966), p. 10.
14. "Editorial," POETRY IRELAND, 3 (Spring, 1964), 92.
15. "Review," THE BELL, 3 (June, 1952), 191.
16. NATIONALISM IN MODERN ANGLO-IRISH POETRY (Madison, 1964), p. 271.
17. OLD-FASHIONED PILGRIMAGE AND OTHER POEMS (Dublin, 1967), p. 25.
18. THE SINGING-MEN AT CASHEL (London, 1936), pp. 168-193.
19. OLD-FASHIONED PILGRIMAGE, p. 55.
20. *Ibid.*, p. 18.
21. FLIGHT TO AFRICA (Dublin, 1963), p. 18.
22. *Ibid.*, p. 26.
23. OLD-FASHIONED PILGRIMAGE, pp. 35-36.
24. *Ibid.*, pp. 34-35.
25. Interview with Austin Clarke on 20 June 1969, Dublin, Ireland.
26. THE ECHO AT COOLE AND OTHER POEMS (Dublin, 1968), p. 41.
27. *Ibid.*, p. 75.
28. *Ibid.*, p. 78.
29. *Ibid.*, p. 26.
30. *Ibid.*, p. 29.
31. *Ibid.*, p. 55.
32. POETRY IRELAND, 3 (Spring, 1964), 92.
33. ECHO, p. 46.
34. Interview with Clarke.
35. (Dublin, 1958), p. 12.
36. *Ibid.*, p. 37.
37. *Ibid.*, p. 14.
38. *Ibid.*, p. 9.
39. DOWNSTREAM (Dublin, 1962), p. 45.
40. Kinsella mentioned this significance when I was talking with him in the Shelbourne Lounge, Dublin, Ireland, 20 June 1969.
41. DOWNSTREAM, p. 63.

42. DOWNSTREAM, p. 56.
43. WORMWOOD (Dublin, 1966), p. 5.
44. *Ibid.*, p. 11.
45. *Ibid.*, p. 7.
46. EIRE-IRELAND, II: 2 (Summer, 1967), 15.
47. *Ibid.*, p. 14.
48. *Ibid.*, p. 15.
49. (Dublin, 1968), p. 14.
50. *Ibid.*, p. 81.
51. *Ibid.*, p. 71.
52. *Ibid.*, p. 66.
53. *Ibid.*, p. 57.
54. *Ibid.*, p. 59.
55. *Ibid.*, p. 50.
56. *Ibid.*, pp. 46-47.
57. *Ibid.*, p. 63.
58. *Ibid.*, p. 74.
59. *Ibid.*, p. 82.
60. EIRE-IRELAND, p. 10.
61. POEMS & TRANSLATIONS (New York, 1961), pp. 71-72.
62. *Ibid.*, p. 73.
63. THE TAIN (Dublin, 1969), p. 255.
64. *Ibid.*, p. 44.
65. *Ibid.*, p. 126.
66. "By the Waters of Babylon," THRESHOLD, IV: 2 (Autumn/Winter), 81.
67. "Off the Barricade: A Note on Three Irish Poets," THE DOLMEN MISCELLANY OF IRISH WRITING (Dublin, 1962), pp. 114-116.
68. THE DARK EDGE OF EUROPE (London, 1967), p. 13.
69. *Ibid.*, p. 15.
70. *Ibid.*, pp. 31-32.
71. *Ibid.*, p. 36.
72. *Ibid.*, p. 49.
73. *Ibid.*, p. 72.
74. (London, 1968), p. 11.
75. *Ibid.*, p. 24.

76. *Ibid.*, p. 18.
77. *Ibid.*, p. 30.
78. *Ibid.*, p. 33.
79. *Ibid.*, p. 47.
80. THE COLLECTED POEMS OF W. B. YEATS (New York, 1959), pp. 184-185.
81. *Ibid.*, p. 50.
82. (Dublin, 1968), p. 9.
83. *Ibid.*, p. 23.
84. *Ibid.*, p. 19.
85. *Ibid.*, p. 29.
86. *Ibid.*, p. 26.
87. *Ibid.*, p. 26.
88. SAILING TO AN ISLAND (London, 1963), p. 43.
89. *Ibid.*, p.38.
90. *Ibid.*, p. 58.
91. *Ibid.*, p. 16.
92. *Ibid.*, pp. 18-19.
93. THE BATTLE OF AUGHRIM AND THE GOD WHO EATS THE CORN (London, 1968), p. 56.
94. *Ibid.*, p. 63.
95. *Ibid.*, p. 11.
96. *Ibid.*, p. 13.
97. *Ibid.*, p. 37.
98. *Ibid.*, p. 46.
99. LADY AND GENTLEMAN (Dublin, 1963), p. 8.
100. *Ibid.*, p. 20.
101. (Dublin, 1968), p. 23.
102. Interview with Richard Weber on 1 July 1969, Ballyknockan, Ireland.
103. STEPHEN'S GREEN REVISITED, p. 17.
104. *Ibid.*, p. 64.
105. *Ibid.*, p. 45.
106. *Ibid.*, p. 60.
107. *Ibid.*
108. (Dublin, 1959), p. 3.
109. *Ibid.*, p. 7.
110. *Ibid.*, p. 13.

111. *Ibid.*, pp. 25, 61.
112. THE IRISH COMIC TRADITION (Oxford, 1962), pp. 47-77.
113. COLLECTION ONE. GETTING UP EARLY (Dublin, 1966), p. 47.
114. *Ibid.*, p. 40.
115. Interview with Brendan Kennelly on 2 July 1969, Dublin, Ireland.
116. DREAM OF A BLACK FOX (Dublin, 1968), p. 55.
117. *Ibid.*, p. 30.
118. *Ibid.*, p. 45.
119. THE RAIN, THE MOON (Dublin, 1961), p. 32.
120. *Ibid.*, p. 29.
121. TRANSLATIONS FROM THE ENGLISH (Dublin, 1965), p. 1.
122. *Ibid.*, p. 28.
123. *Ibid.*, p. 35.
124. (Leeds, 1967).
125. *Ibid.*
126. Interview with Rudi Holzapfel on 14 June 1969, Leeds, England.
127. Interview with Rudi Holzapfel.
128. Four issues have been published by the Dolmen Press for the Poetry Workshop UCD.

*Chapter VI*

1. THRESHOLD, V: 1 (Spring/Summer, 1961), 5.
2. THRESHOLD, V: 2 (Autumn/Winter), 59-74.
3. "Recent Verse by Irish Poets," THRESHOLD, II: 2 (Summer, 1958), 72.
4. "The Cobbler's Song," THRESHOLD, V: 1 (Spring/Summer, 1961), 51.
5. "Men from the Fields," THRESHOLD, IV: 1 (Autumn/Winter, 1960-1961), 66.
6. THE COLLECTED POEMS OF JOHN HEWITT (London, 1968), p. 69.
7. *Ibid.*, p. 144.
8. *Ibid.*, p. 5.

9. *Ibid.*, p. 83.
10. *Ibid.*, p. 61.
11. *Ibid.*, pp. 64-65.
12. *Ibid.*, p. 22.
13. *Ibid.*, p. 53.
14. *Ibid.*, p. 14.
15. *Ibid.*, p. 110.
16. *Ibid.*, pp. 95-96.
17. *Ibid.*, p. 130.
18. *Ibid.*, pp. 119-120, 128.
19. *Ibid.*, p. 123.
20. "Reflections on Megarrity," THRESHOLD, V: 1 (Spring-Summer, 1961), 25.
21. FLOWERS FOR A LADY (London, 1945), p. 22.
22. *Ibid.*, p. 48.
23. *Ibid.*, p. 13.
24. *Ibid.*, pp. 52-58.
25. HEART'S TOWNLAND, (London, 1947), p. 25.
26. THRESHOLD, II: 2 (Summer, 1958), 19.
27. Letter from John Montague dated January 1970, Paris, France.
28. "The Young Writer," THE BELL, VII: 7 (October, 1951), 6.
29. (Dublin, 1958), pp. 22-23.
30. (London, 1967), p. 16.
31. Interview with John Montague on 21 July 1969, Paris, France.
32. IV: 2 (Autumn/Winter, 1960), 74.
33. After its publication in THRESHOLD, Montague published this poem in POISONED LANDS (London, 1957), p. 19.
34. *Ibid.*, p. 36.
35. POISONED LANDS, p. 25.
36. *Ibid.*, pp. 27-28.
37. Interview with John Montague.
38. POISONED LANDS, p. 15.
39. CHOSEN LIGHT, p. 51.
40. *Ibid.*, p. 52.
41. *Ibid.*, p. 71.
42. *Ibid.*, p. 22.

43. *Ibid.*, p. 50.
44. THE ROUGH FIELD (Dublin, 1972), p. 73.
45. *Ibid.*, p. 74.
46. IRELAND OF THE WELCOMES, XVII: 5 (January/February, 1969), 18.
47. *Ibid.*, p. 18.
48. *Ibid.*, p. 19.
49. Interview with John Montague.
50. THE BREAD GOD (Dublin, 1968), title page.
51. *Ibid.*, p. vi.
52. *Ibid.*, p. viii.
53. *Ibid.*, p. ix.
54. Interview with John Montague.
55. THE ROUGH FIELD, p. 53.
56. (Dublin, August, 1970), cover.
57. *Ibid.*, text.
58. *Ibid.*
59. TIDES (Dublin, 1970), p. 11.
60. *Ibid.*, p. 26.
61. *Ibid.*, p. 27.
62. *Ibid.*, pp. 39-42.
63. *Ibid.*, p. 64.
64. (London, 1967).
65. No. 23 (Summer, 1970), 1.
66. *Ibid.*, 29-37.
67. *Ibid.*, 38-44.
68. *Ibid.*, 3-4.
69. THE SUNDAY PRESS (July 12, 1970).
70. No. 22 (Summer, 1969), 3.

### Chapter VII

1. THE HONEST ULSTERMAN, 16 (August, 1969), 23-24.
2. THE HONEST ULSTERMAN, 18 (October, 1969), 2.
3. *Ibid.*
4. *Ibid.*, p. 54.
5. THE HONEST ULSTERMAN, 11 (March, 1969), 3.
6. THE HONEST ULSTERMAN, 2 (June, 1968), 11.
7. (Belfast, n.d.), p. 2.
8. *Ibid.*, p. 6.

9. (London, 1967), p. 38.
10. *Ibid.*, p. 43.
11. *Ibid.*, p. 14.
12. *Ibid.*, p. 24.
13. THE HONEST ULSTERMAN, 1 (May,1968), 20.
14. *Ibid.*, p. 21.
15. THE HONEST ULSTERMAN, 2 (June,1968), 14.
16. *Ibid.*, p. 15.
17. No. 11 (April,1969), 2.
18. *Ibid.*, p. 7.
19. THE HONEST ULSTERMAN, 14 (June,1968), 16.
20. THE HONEST ULSTERMAN, 13 (May,1969), 30-34.
21. *Ibid.*, p. 2.
22. HEIL HITLER (Portrush, 1969), p. 2.
23. *Ibid.*, p. 5.
24. THE HONEST ULSTERMAN, 21 (January/February, 1970), 45.
25. THE HONEST ULSTERMAN, 19 (November, 1969), 16.
26. THE HONEST ULSTERMAN, 21 (January/February, 1970), 4-5.
27. THE HONEST ULSTERMAN, 11 (March, 1969), 2.
28. THE HONEST ULSTERMAN, 8 (December, 1969), 13.
29. DEATH OF A NATURALIST (London, 1968), p. 23.
30. *Ibid.*, p. 16.
31. *Ibid.*
32. *Ibid.*, p. 31.
33. DOOR INTO THE DARK (London, 1969), p. 21.
34. DEATH OF A NATURALIST, p. 41.
35. *Ibid.*, p. 53.
36. P. 23.
37. *Ibid.*, p. 49.
38. Letter from Seamus Heaney dated 26 March 1970, Belfast, Northern Ireland. Back cover of THE NORTHERN MUSE (Dublin: Claddagh Records, 1969).
39. Mimeograph copy, undated.
40. Letter from Seamus Heaney.
41. Mimeograph copy.
42. "Patrick Kavanagh. A Tribute in Poetry and Prose," THE DUBLIN MAGAZINE, VII: 1 (1968), 8.

43. NIGHT-CROSSING (London, 1968), p. 3.
44. Interview with Derek Mahon on 15 August 1969, Dublin, Ireland.
45. *Ibid.*
46. NIGHT-CROSSING, p. 9.
47. *Ibid.*, p. 33.
48. *Ibid.*, p. 29.
49. *Ibid.*, p. 6.
50. "NIGHT-CROSSING by Derek Mahon," THE HONEST ULSTERMAN, 8 (December, 1968), 27.
51. NIGHT-CROSSING, p. 19.
52. "NIGHT-CROSSING by Derek Mahon," p. 28.
53. No. 1 (March, 1970), 5.
54. Interview with Derek Mahon.
55. "Burke and Machiavelli," ATLANTIS, 1 (March, 1970), 7-17.
56. (October, 1970), 8.
57. Gustav Mayer, FRIEDRICH ENGELS. A BIOGRAPHY (London, 1936), pp. 192-193.

*Chapter VIII*

1. (Dublin, 1971), pp. 73-74.
2. *Ibid.*, p. 57.
3. *Ibid.*, p. 21.
4. *Ibid.*, pp. 71-72.
5. *Ibid.*, p. 29.
6. *Ibid.*, p. 71.
7. THE LACE CURTAIN, 4 (Summer, 1971), 61.
8. SELECTED POEMS (Dublin, 1971), p. 55.
9. *Ibid.*, p. 15.
10. *Ibid.*, p. 63.
11. *Ibid.*, p. 30.
12. *Ibid.*, p. 31.
13. *Ibid.*
14. COLLECTED POEMS (Dublin, 1973), p. 26.
15. *Ibid.*, pp. 56-57.
16. T. S. Eliot, "The Hollow Men," THE COMPLETE POEMS AND PLAYS, 1909-1950 (New York, 1952), p. 56.
17. COLLECTED POEMS, p. 23.

18. *Ibid.*, p. 58.
19. *Ibid.*, p. 62.
20. *Ibid.*, p. 71.
21. *Ibid.*, p. 72.
22. *Ibid.*, p. 73.
23. *Ibid.*, p. 84.
24. (Dublin, 1971), p. 2.
25. *Ibid.*, p. 6.
26. *Ibid.*, p. 1.
27. TAO (Dublin, 1971), p. 18.
28. T. S. Eliot, "Tradition and the Individual Talent," SELECTED ESSAYS, (London, 1958), pp. 13-14.
29. SELECTED POEMS (Dublin, 1970), pp. 53, 61.
30. *Ibid.*, p. 19.
31. *Ibid.*, p. 29.
32. *Ibid.*, p. 38.
33. (Dublin, 1970), pp. 8, 6-7.
34. *Ibid.*, pp. 9, 10-11.
35. *Ibid.*, p. 19.
36. Samuel Johnson, LIVES OF THE ENGLISH POETS, ed. George Birkbeck Hill (New York, 1967), I, 20.
37. PENTAHEDRON (Dublin, 1972), p. 31.
38. *Ibid.*, p. 12.
39. *Ibid.*, p. 44.
40. ON LOANING HILL (Dublin, 1972), dustcover.
41. *Ibid.*, p. 75.
42. *Ibid.*, pp. 15, 45.
43. *Ibid.*, p. 45.
44. (Dublin, 1971), II.
45. *Ibid.*, II.
46. (Dublin, 1971), p. 24.
47. (Dublin, 1971), 11, pp. 44-45, 54-61.

### Chapter IX

1. Conversation with Allen Ginsberg, April, 1970, San Antonio, Texas.
2. POEMS IN ENGLISH (New York, 1961), p. 13.

# Bibliography
## of Books Cited

Bardwell, Leland.  THE MAD CYCLIST. Dublin: New Writer's Press, 1970.

Beckett, Samuel.  POEMS IN ENGLISH. New York: Grove, 1961.

Bergson, Henri.  CREATIVE EVOLUTION. New York: Greenwood, 1946.

Auden, W. H.  THE COLLECTED POETRY OF W. H. AUDEN. New York: Random House, 1945.

    . THE SELECTED POETRY OF W. H. AUDEN. New York: Random House, 1970.

Carroll, Donald, ed.  NEW POETS OF IRELAND. Denver: Swallow, 1963.

Clarke, Austin.  THE COLLECTED POEMS OF AUSTIN CLARKE. London: Allen and Unwin, 1936.

    . THE ECHO AT COOLE AND OTHER POEMS. Dublin: Dolmen, 1968.

    . FLIGHT TO AFRICA. Dublin: Dolmen, 1963.

    . OLD-FASHIONED PILGRIMAGE AND OTHER POEMS. Dublin: Dolmen, 1967.

    . POETRY IN MODERN IRELAND. Dublin: Sign of the Three Candles, 1951.

    . POETRY IN MODERN IRELAND. Rev. ed. Cork: Mercier, (n.d.)

    . POETRY IN MODERN IRELAND. Cork: Mercier, (n.d.).

    . THE SINGING-MEN AT CASHEL. London: Allen and Unwin, 1936.

Coffey, Brian.  SELECTED POEMS. Dublin: New Writer's Press, 1971.

Cronin, Anthony.  POEMS. London: Cresset, 1957.

    . COLLECTED POEMS. Dublin: New Writer's Press, 1973.

Devlin, Denis.  COLLECTED POEMS. Dublin: Dolmen, 1964.

    . THE HEAVENLY FOREIGNER. Dublin: Dolmen, 1967.

    . SELECTED POEMS. Ed. by Allan Tate and Robert Penn Warren. New York: Holt, Rinehart, and Winston, 1963.

Eliade, Mircea.  COSMOS AND HISTORY. New York: Harper, 1971.

Eliot, T. S.  THE COMPLETE POEMS AND PLAYS, 1909-1950. New York: Harcourt, Brace & World, 1952.

    . SELECTED ESSAYS. London: Faber and Faber, 1958.

Foley, Michael.  HEIL HITLER. Portrrush: Ulsterman Publications, 1969.

Graves, Robert.  COLLECTED POEMS. New York: Doubleday, 1966.

Hartnett, Michael.  TAO. Dublin: New Writer's Press, 1971.

    . ANATOMY OF A CLICHÉ. Dublin: Dolmen, 1968.

    . SELECTED POEMS. Dublin: New Writer's Press, 1970.

Heaney, Seamus. DEATH OF A NATURALIST. London: Faber and Faber, 1968.

191

.   DOOR INTO THE DARK. London: Faber and Faber, 1969.
Hewitt, John.   THE COLLECTED POEMS OF JOHN HEWITT. London:
    MacGibbon and Kee, 1968.
Holzapfel, Rudi.   FOR LOVE OF IRELAND. Leeds: Pvt. Ptd., 1967.
.   TRANSLATIONS FROM THE ENGLISH. Dublin: At the
    Museum Bookshop, 1965.
        and Brendan Kennelly.   *the rain, the moon*. Dublin: Dolmen, 1961.
.   CAST A COLD EYE. Dublin: Dolmen, 1959.
Hutchinson, Pearse.   EXPANSIONS. Dublin: Dolmen, 1969.
.   TONGUE WITHOUT HANDS. Dublin: Dolmen, 1963.
Iremonger, Valentin.   RESERVATIONS. Dublin: Envoy, 1950.
        , ed.   IRISH SHORT STORES. London: Faber and Faber, 1960.
Johnson, Samuel.   LIVES OF THE ENGLISH POETS. Ed. George Birkbeck
    Hill. New York: Octagon Books, 1967.
Jordan, John.   PATRICIAN STATIONS. Dublin: New Writer's Press, 1971.
Joyce, James.   A PORTRAIT OF THE ARTIST AS A YOUNG MAN. New
    York: Viking, 1965.
Joyce, Trevor.   PENTAHEDRON. Dublin: New Writer's Press, 1972.
Kavanagh, Patrick.   COLLECTED POEMS. New York: Devin-Adair, 1964.
Kennelly, Brendan.   COLLECTION ONE. GETTING UP EARLY. Dublin: A.
    Figgis, 1966.
.   DREAM OF A BLACK FOX. Dublin: A. Figgis, 1968.
Kinsella, Thomas.   ANOTHER SEPTEMBER. Dublin: Dolmen, 1958.
.   DOWNSTREAM. Dublin: Dolmen, 1962.
.   NIGHTWALKER. Dublin: Dolmen, 1968.
.   POEMS AND TRANSLATIONS. New York: Atheneum, 1961.
.   THE TAIN. Dublin: Dolmen, 1969.
.   WORMWOOD. Dublin: Dolmen, 1966.
Liddy, James.   ESSAU MY KINGDOM FOR A DRINK. Dublin: Dolmen,
    1962.
.   IN A BLUE SMOKE. Dublin: Dolmen, 1964.
.   HOMAGE TO PATRICK KAVANAGH. Dublin: New Writer's
    Press, 1971.
Loftus, Richard.   NATIONALISM IN MODERN ANGLO-IRISH POETRY.
    Madison: University of Wisconsin, 1964.
MacGreevy, Thomas.   COLLECTED POEMS. Dublin: New Writer's Press,
    1971.
McFadden, Roy.   FLOWERS FOR A LADY. London: Routledge, 1945.
.   HEART'S TOWNLAND. London: Routledge, 1947.
Mahon, Derek.   NIGHT-CROSSING. London: Oxford, 1968.
Meyer, Gustav.   FRIEDRICH ENGELS. A BIOGRAPHY. London: Fertig,
    1936.
Mercier, Vivian.   THE IRISH COMIC TRADITION. Oxford: Clarendon,
    1962.
Miller, Liam and John Montague.   A TRIBUTE TO AUSTIN CLARKE ON
    HIS SEVENTIETH BIRTHDAY. Dublin: Dolmen, 1966.
Milne, Ewart.   DIAMOND CUT DIAMOND. London: Bodley Head, 1950.

.   A GARLAND FOR THE GREEN. London: Hutchinson, 1962.

.   GALION. Dublin: Dolmen, 1953.

.   LISTEN MANGAN. Dublin: Sign of the Three Candles, 1941.

.   JUBILO. London: Muller, 1944.

.   ONCE MORE TO TOURNEY. London: Linden, 1958.

.   TIME STOPPED. London: Plow Poems, 1967.

Montague, John.   THE BREAD GOD. Dublin: Dolmen, 1968.

.   A CHOSEN LIGHT. London: MacGibbon and Kee, 1967.

.   A NEW SIEGE. Dublin: Dolmen, 1970.

.   DEATH OF A CHIEFTAIN. N.p.: Dufour, 1967.

.   FORMS OF EXILE. Dublin: Dolmen, 1958.

.   POISONED LANDS. London: MacGibbon and Kee, 1957.

.   THE ROUGH FIELD. Dublin: Dolmen, 1972.

.   TIDES. Dublin: Dolmen, 1970.

and Thomas Kinsella, eds.   THE DOLMEN MISCELLANY OF IRISH WRITING. Dublin: Dolmen, 1962.

Murphy, Richard.   THE BATTLE OF AUGHRIM AND THE GOD WHO EATS THE CORN. London: Faber and Faber, 1968.

.   SAILING TO AN ISLAND. London: Faber and Faber, 1963.

Murray, Paul.   RITUAL POEMS. Dublin: New Writer's Press, 1971.

Neumann, Eric.   ART AND THE CREATIVE UNCONSCIOUS. New York: Harper, 1959.

O'Grady, Desmond.   DARK EDGE OF EUROPE. London: MacGibbon and Kee, 1967.

.   THE DYING GAUL. London: MacGibbon and Kee, 1968.

.   OFF LICENSE. Dublin: Dolmen, 1968.

.   HELLAS. Dublin: New Writer's Press, 1971.

Plath, Sylvia.   ARIEL. London: Faber and Faber, 1967.

Podhoretz, Norman.   MAKING IT. New York: Random, 1967.

Simmons, James.   BALLAD OF A MARRIAGE. (Belfast): Queens University, (n.d.).

.   LATE BUT IN EARNEST. London: The Bodley Head, 1967.

Weber, Richard.   LADY AND GENTLEMAN. Dublin: Dolmen, 1963.

.   STEPHEN'S GREEN REVISITED. Dublin: Dolmen, 1968.

Yeats, William Butler.   THE AUTOBIOGRAPHY OF WILLIAM BUTLER YEATS. Garden City: Doubleday, 1958.

.   THE COLLECTED POEMS OF W. B. YEATS. New York: Macmillan, 1959.

Young, Augustus.   ON LOANING HILL. Dublin: New Writer's Press, 1972.

# Index

## M

MacBeth, George, 48, 161
MacDonagh, Donagh, 48
McFadden, Roy, 18, 59, 115-117
MacGreevy, Thomas, 153-155
MacNeice, Louis, 51, 64, 87, 148, 149, 151
Madden, P. J., 39
Mahon, Derek, 132, 133, 148-152, 172
Malcolm X, 139
Mangan, James Clarence, 106
Marckewitz, Constance, 27
Marcus, David, 40, 50-52, 60, 61
Marx, Karl, 152
Mercier, Vivian, 102
Metaphor, 4, 9, 16, 47, 80, 81, 100, 101, 119, 154, 164-166, 170
Miller, Henry, 8
Miller, Liam, 62, 63, 85, 106, 107
Milne, Edward, 37, 41-51
Molloy, 151
Montague, John, 3, 18, 19, 35, 37, 59, 60, 66, 110, 117-134, 143, 147, 149, 160, 171, 172
Moore, Brian, 2-3, 131-132
Moore, George, 30
Morgan, Pete, 139, 140
Muldoon, Paul, 132
Murphy, Richard, 93-98, 160, 161, 171
Murray, Paul, 166, 167

## N

naGopaleen, Myles (Brian O'Nolan), 2
Nash, Ogden, 46
Neumann, Erich, 53

## O

O'Brien, Conor Cruise, 148, 152
O'Cassey, Sean, 11, 32, 33, 41, 48
O'Connor, Frank, 42, 102
O'Faolain, Sean, 51

THIS BOOK WAS DESIGNED BY
JUDITH M. OELFKE
SET IN TEN-POINT GARAMOND
BY FORT WORTH LINOTYPING COMPANY
AND PRINTED ON WARREN'S OLDE STYLE WOVE
BY MOTHERAL PRINTING COMPANY